Asian Pressure Cooker Cookbook

Easy and Healthy Asian Multicooker Recipes Made Fast with Your Electric Pressure Cooker

Over 120 Chicken, Beef, Noodle, Vegetarian Meals in One Book

Tiffany Shelton

Copyright © 2020 by Tiffany Shelton.

All rights reserved.

No part of this book may be reproduced in any form or by any electronic or mechanical means, except in the case of a brief quotation embodied in articles or reviews, without written permission from its publisher.

Disclaimer

The recipes and information in this book are provided for educational purposes only. Please always consult a licensed professional before making changes to your lifestyle or diet. The author and publisher shall have neither liability nor responsibility to anyone with respect to any loss or damage caused or alleged to be caused directly or indirectly by the information contained in this book. All trademarks and brands within this book are for clarifying purposes only and are owned by the owners themselves, not affiliated with this document.

Images from shutterstock.com

CONTENTS

INTRODUCTION 9

CHAPTER 1. Diversity of Asian Cuisines 10

    Japanese cuisine 10

    Chinese cuisine 11

    Vietnamese cuisine 11

    Indian cuisine 12

    Korean cuisine 13

    Thai cuisine 14

    Singaporean cuisine 14

    Malaysian cuisine 15

CHAPTER 2. Asian pantry essentials 16

    Basics 16

    Spices 17

    Sauces 19

CHAPTER 3. Recipes 21

SAUCES AND SPICES 21

    Thai Sweet Chili Sauce 21

    Ginger Sauce 22

    Teriyaki Sauce 23

    Hoisin Sauce 24

    Chinese Lemon Sauce 25

    Gochujang – Korean Red Chili Sauce 26

    Chinese 5 Spice Mix 27

    Garam Masala 28

    Chai Spice Mix 29

    Curry Powder 30

BREAKFAST 31

    Eight Treasure Congee 31

    Nikujaga – Japanese Stewed Beef and Potatoes 32

    Congee with Bacon and Egg 33

    Quinoa Breakfast Bowl 34

    Takikomi Gohan – Japanese Mixed Rice 35

    Black Rice Pudding 36

    Chawanmushi – Steamed Egg Custard 37

    Mushroom Ramekin Eggs 38

Miso Oatmeal 39
Pork Pho with Bacon 40

SOUPS ANS STEWS 41

Ramen Soup 41
Pork Belly Ramen 42
Miso Soup 43
Kimchi Jjigae 44
Sundubu Jjigae 45
Red Lentil Soup 46
Shrimp Tom Kha 47
Bak Kut Teh – Pork Ribs Soup 48
Laksa Soup 49
Galbitang – Short Ribs Soup 50
Miyeok Guk – Seaweed Soup 51
Chinese Pork Shoulder Soup 52

CHICKEN 53

Teriyaki Chicken 53
Teriyaki Wings 54
Korean Gochujang Sticky Chicken Wings 55
Thai Lemongrass Chicken 56
Cashew Chicken 57
Tandoori Chicken 58
Mango Chicken 59
General Tso Chicken 60
Kung Pao Chicken 61
Chicken Tikka Masala 62
Orange Chicken Lettuce Wraps 63

MEAT 64

Hibachi Steak and Vegetables 64
Korean Beef 65
Korean Short Ribs 66
Yukgaejang 67
Massaman Beef Curry 68
Vietnamese Beef Pho 69
Vietnamese Bo Kho 70
Caramelized Pork 71
Banh Mi 72

Beef Rendang 73
Szechuan Beef 74
Char Siu – Chinese BBQ Pork 75
Indian Curry Lamb 76
Bacon Ramen 77

FISH & SEAFOOD 78

Vietnamese Salmon 78
Shrimp Tempura 79
Chao Ca – Vietnamese Fish Congee 80
Coconut Caramel Shrimp 81
Vietnamese Caramel Salmon 82
Coconut Mahi-Mahi 83
Indian Butter Shrimp 84
Asaam Pedas Fish 85
Steamed Sea Bass 86
Steamed Fish with Ginger 87
Panko-Crusted Cod 88
Sambal Udang – Prawn Sandal 89
Shrimp with Lobster Sauce 90

RICE & NOODLES 91

Japanese Fried Rice 91
Hibachi Fried Rice 92
Chicken Pad Thai 93
Chicken Rice Bowls 94
Bang Bang Shrimp Pasta 95
Chao Ga – Vietnamese Chicken Congee 96
Hainanese Chicken Rice 97
Nasi Lemak – Malay Coconut Milk Rice 98
Singapore Curry Noodles 99
Congee 100
Chili Garlic Noodles 101
Lo Mein Beef and Broccoli 102
Rice Pilaf 103
Rice and Vegetables 104
Honey Sesame Chicken Noodles 105

LENTILS, GRAINS AND BEANS 106

Thai Lentil Chickpea Curry 106

Creamy Red Curry Lentil	107
Chana Masala	108
Red Lentil and Potato Curry	109
Lentil Dal	110
Green Beans Potato Curry	111
Kung Pao Chickpeas	112
Japgokbap – Multigrain Rice	113
Southern Green Beans	114
Khidhi – Rice and Lentil Porridge	115

VEGETARIAN MEALS 116

Thai Green Curry with Tofu	116
Lentil and Sweet Potato Thai Curry	117
Split Pea Soup	118
Vegetable Chow Mein	119
Chinese Kale	120
Vegan White Bean Kale Soup	121
Indian Saag Tofu	122
Vegetable Pho Noodle Soup	123
Udon Soup	124
Pad Thai	125

DESSERTS 126

Tsubu-An – Red Bean Paste	126
Yaksik – Sticky Rice Dessert	127
Tapioca Pudding	128
Japanese Cotton Cheesecake	129
Jello Mochi	130
Chana Dal Kheer	131
Gajar Halwa	132
Kakaland	133
Chinese Turnip Cake	134
Nian Gao – Chinese New Year Cake	135

DRINKS 136

Boba Tea	136
Sikhye – Korean Rice Drink	137
Nourishing Chinese Red Dates Tea	138
Suanmeitang – Sour Plum Drink	139
Chai Tea	140

Barley Winter Melon Drink 141
Amazake – Japanese Rice Drink 142
Indian Masala Milk 143
Aam Panna – Raw Mango Drink 144
Shikandji – Indian Lemonade 145
CONCLUSION 146
Recipe Index 147
Conversion Tables 149
Other Books by Tiffany Shelton 150

INTRODUCTION

If you're reading this, you probably have those two things: Instant Pot and interest in the Asian cuisine, if so this book is for you. With our book, the combination of those two things won't be a headache anymore – in fact, vice versa complexity will turn to simplicity. How's that going to happen? This Instant Pot cookbook combines pressure cooking with Asian dishes to make them so much quicker to make, yet easier to cook, and even tastier to eat.

So why Asian Instant Pot cookbook? Because any Asian cuisine is perfect for Instant Pot. We all know that most parts of Asian recipes take a lot of time to get the deep taste and flavor. And you can't even be distracted by something else while cooking! The pressure cooker will make your life more relaxed and save you a lot of time. You can cook meat, soups, and broth while doing other activities. The meat will fall off the bone easily, and it will make your fish edible and tender. You can be sure that Instant Pot will make your meals not only tastier but it will also make it quicker, and maintain the nutrition in the food.

CHAPTER 1. Diversity of Asian Cuisines

Nowadays, traditional Asian cuisine is one of the most popular cuisines in the world. We love Thai food, Chinese food, Japanese food, Indian food, and others. It's delicious and has a unique taste, different from other food. Many dishes are easily prepared, and cooked from cheap ingredients that you can find in most food-stores. It's perfect and easy for everyone!

Japanese cuisine

The main two ingredients of Japanese cuisine are rice and noodles. Rice can be boiled or steamed and is served at every meal. The diversity of noodles is impressive: soba (thin brown noodles) made from buckwheat flour; udon (thick white noodles) and ramen (thin, curly noodles) made from wheat flour. Don't forget about the other staple – soybean products and especially soy sauce. In the Japanese kitchen, it's easy to find other ingredients such as bamboo shoots, daikon radish, ginger, seaweed, and sesame seed products. As it is an island nation, seafood is a huge part of Japanese food. Depending on the region, Japanese people also enjoy corn, potatoes, and barbecued meats. The Japanese cook their meals from fresh seasonal ingredients on the same day they bought it. Japanese food is also famous for its beautiful arrangement, which is one of the traditional requirements of Japanese cooking.

Chinese cuisine

Chinese food has its own style and traditions. Stir-frying, deep-frying, and pan-frying are common cooking techniques for this country. Rice and noodles are the main components of each dish. China is large enough to create different regional preferences, for example the northern people use wheat for cooking noodles, while the southern people chose rice as their favorite grain. For cooking meats, they use poultry and pork. Vegetables, especially cabbage, fruit, eggs, Tofu, fish, and shellfish and are also popular among Chinese people. A typical recipe for a home meal includes soup, boiled rice, steamed fish, and stir-fried pork with vegetables. When they cook individual dishes, they are trying to create harmony between flavors and texture of ingredients.

Vietnamese cuisine

Com Trang or lactose plain rice is the key to Vietnamese dishes. While Chinese people prefer short-grain rice for their cooking, the Vietnamese use this long-grain white rice as a common component of almost every meal. Rice also enables the production of other foods such as rice wine, rice vinegar, and rice paper wrappers for spring rolls. Rice can be used to make the three main types of noodles: banh pho (wide white noodles) are used for Vietnamese soup, pho; bun noodles (rice vermicelli); banh hoi is a thinner version of bun noodles. You can find noodles made from mung bean starch.

Nuoc mam or a salty fish sauce is as essential to Vietnamese cooking as rice or noodles are. It's used as a major part of Vietnamese dishes. Nuoc Mam is a kind of salt in Western cuisine. The second most popular sauce is Nuoc Cham or dipping sauce, which is widely used among Vietnamese people and serves as the main filling for every meal, for dipping everything from spring rolls to meatballs into it. During dinner, you will always find your saucer filled with Nuoc Cham.

Indian cuisine

Indian food is known as one of the most delicious and unique foods in the culinary world. Its main purpose is to create harmony between spices and herbs in every meal. Surprisingly, Indian dishes can be used for medicinal needs thanks to their features. Indian food doesn't have only one flavor. The large size of the country is the main cause of the individual cooking traditions from every region. The diverseness of food taste between East and West or North and South made India one of the most popular tourist countries. You won't find a person who wasn't impressed with this wealth of flavors. Culinary diversity is one of India's treasures. Each area has its distinctive culinary features and a wide variety of traditional dishes.

One of the most popular Indian cooking techniques which gains more and more lovers around the world every year is the famous Tandoori. The meat, fish or bread is marinated and macerated in spicy and flavored yogurt then barbecued in Indian Tandoori style. The features of dishes, cooked in this way, are amazing. It allows you to create a healthy (fat-free) and tasty meal, which looks very colorful and seduces you while you are looking at it.

For curries, or very spicy sauces in other words, you have to look south. Spicy and curry soups or stew go with vegetables, rice or meat. We are able cook such a wholesome meal thanks to the enormous amount of spices and hot peppers which have a unique taste and the opportunity to experiment with them.

The state of Tamil Nadu is well-known for its simple but delicious dishes - Dhals. Vegetarian dishes that consist of tamarind combined with different lentils and spices. This recipe creates an aromatic meal with a deep taste.

Korean cuisine

Rice is the main staple of Korean food too. It is also an essential part of every meal. In Korea, a common meal consists of a bowl of rice, a few side dishes, pap, and panchan. Some side dishes might be soup, kimchi, vegetables, and fish with sauces such as doenjang, soybean paste, red pepper paste. Also, don't forget about kimchi, the national dish of Korea, which has survived for centuries. The food diversity of Korean meals can be shown with the side dishes served.

The second most important part of Korean meals is soup, kuk, or t'ang. The essential ingredients for soup are fish, meat, and vegetables. For example, Korean soups are kalbi-tang, a beef soup with a deep taste and flavor; mandu-guk, soup with meat dumplings; miyok-kuk, breakfast soup with; tubu chige, a spicy stew cooked with tofu and red pepper paste; mae'unt'ang, a fish soup that includes white fish, scallions, tubu, vegetables, kochujang, and egg.

Thai cuisine

Most dishes include beef, pork, chicken, and seafood. Thai food is well-known for its special combinations of spices. Even though they like hot and spicy food, being carefully cooked, Thai cuisine is balanced to reveal all the diversity of flavors in a dish. Plant-Rice is the key staple of Thai food culture. It is the base for almost every meal, and rice-wheat is used to make dumplings, noodles, and desserts. Curries are also a staple dish of Thai cooking. Other crowd favorites are fish sauce, lemongrass, hot chilies, dried shrimp paste, and among the spices commonly used here are cardamom, coriander, cumin, basil, garlic, ginger, and cinnamon. Soup is served with most meals and helps balance the hot spiciness of Thai dishes. This is the main goal of steamed rice and mild noodle dishes too. Thai food preferences are divided from one region to another. For example, seafood is found in the southern coastal areas. The closer you are to the north east, the spicier the food is.

Singaporean cuisine

Singaporean cuisine includes a huge variety of different ethnic groups that exist as result of Singapore becoming one of the important international seaports and a center of a large immigrant population. Thanks to it, influences include the cuisines of the largest ethnic group, the Chinese, Indonesian, Indian, Peranakan, and the native Malays. There are also influences from regions such as Thailand, Sri Lanka, and the Middle East.

We can talk about five types of Singaporean food: seafood, meat, noodles, rice, and dessert or snacks. Singapore's food culture is especially plentiful with seafood. Two important dishes that dominate the scene are chili crab and black pepper crab, and they are always recommended to tourists. One more favorite dish is the sambal stingray. What about the meat dishes? Hainanese chicken rice is the most popular one. It is rice prepared with chicken fat and served with boiled chicken and chili sauce.

Malaysian cuisine

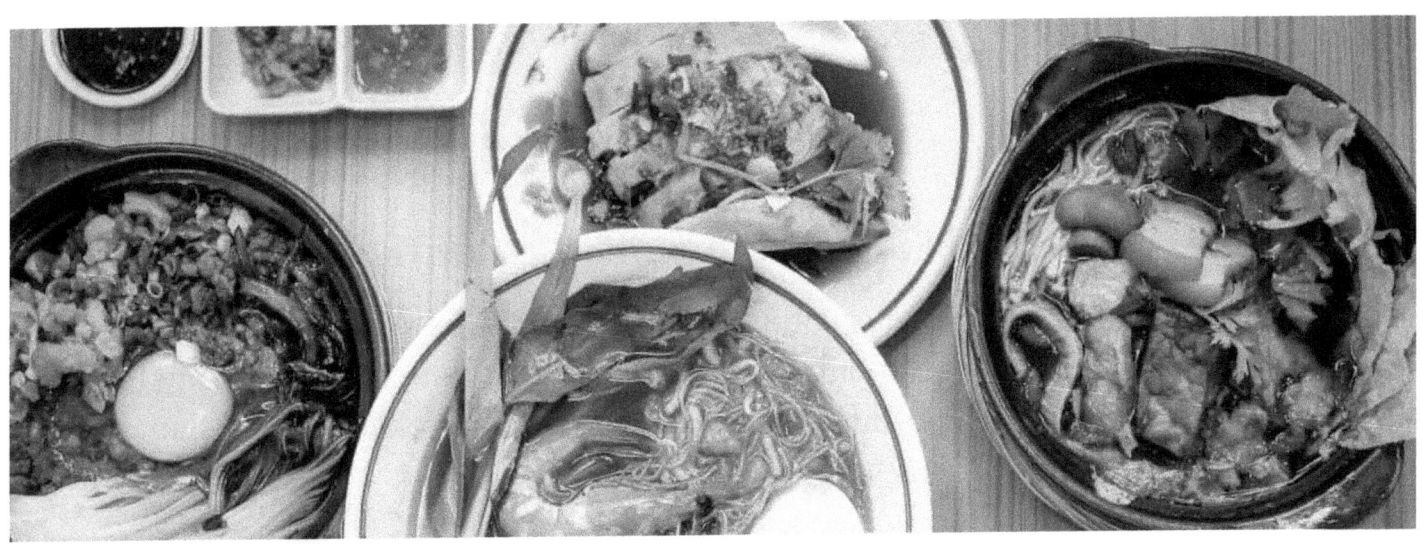

The main grain in Malaysia is rice, just like in other Asian countries. Due to favorable climatic conditions all year round, fruits and vegetables can be easily bought at any time while poultry, meat, and seafood are always fresh, cheap, and readily available. Malaysian food, because of the ethnic diversity, can be divided into Chinese, Malay and Indian, and each is cooked in unique ways.

Malaysian food uses herbs such as lemongrass, tamarind, dried and fresh chilies, ginger and garlic. Malay meals can be divided into several tastes: masak lemak - coconut milk, masak pedas – spicy, masak merah - tomato sauce, masak asam - sourish tamarind. It worth mentioning popular dishes such as nasi lemak (coconut milk steamed rice), also sambal belacan (shrimp paste with pounded chilies), serunding (beef floss) and beef rending (dried curry). Barbecue meat on a stick, or Satay, comes from Malay cuisine and is widely found in restaurants around the world today.

CHAPTER 2. Asian pantry essentials

There are so many different cuisines within Asia, and luckily there is some overlap with the ingredients, which means you can build an arsenal in your pantry and be ready for many kinds of meals. For well balanced, nutritious, and flavorful dishes, keep these Asian products in your pantry at all times!

Basics

<u>Sesame Oil</u> has an amazing nutty flavor that can make the taste of any dish deeper. It works well for frying when added to another type of vegetable oil. It can be used for marinating and making dressing and marinades to give the ingredients a bigger flavor.

<u>Chili oil.</u> A lot of Asian cuisines add spiciness to their dishes, so if you want to create the traditional taste of Asia, you need to keep something spicy like chili oil in your pantry. You can replace it with chili paste, but you should have at least one.

<u>Noodles.</u> Asian noodles can be produced from rice, buckwheat, yam, sweet-potato starch wheat, and mung bean. You can easily find types of noodles such as wheat-based lo mein, udon noodles, rice vermicelli, chow fun, and jap che.

<u>Rice</u> is the main grain across Asia, and it is a #1 must-have for any pantry. It's better to use plain long-grain white rice at first, but then you can experiment with short-grain, brown, basmati, and jasmine as you want.

<u>Rice wine.</u> Analogous in Asian cuisines to using white or red wine for European

dishes. It brings an aromatic note to your marinades, sauces, and different meals.

<u>Rice Vinegar</u> isn't as acidic as other types of vinegar, and thanks to this feature it's more palatable and easier to use. It has a light sweet taste and makes soups and pickled dishes tastier.

<u>Green Beans.</u> The green gram beans have a pleasant taste, and they can be used in curries, soups, and salads. It is the perfect lentil for cooking healthy rice or daal dishes. They can be easily found with and without skin on at the supermarkets or food-store.

<u>Black Eyed Beans</u> are an excellent ingredient as a base for a delicious curry. At first, you need to soak them for 5-6 hours before cooking your curry.

<u>Red Lentils and Split Red Lentils.</u> The type of lentils that are widely found across Asia. It's the most popular choice for curries, soups, rice and breakfast bowls. Split red lentils are good for tasty daal. You can find this type of lentil in almost every grocery store.

Spices

If you want to make an authentic Asian meal with its traditional taste and flavor, you need to spice it! What spices do you need for cooking? Let's start with lemongrass, coriander, cumin, ginger, turmeric, cardamom, fenugreek, and black pepper. We won't talk about salt, because no cuisine can go without it.

Lemongrass comes from India and tropical Asia. It is a tall, perennial grass with a citrus flavor that goes well with meat in Thai meals. It is commonly used with tempeh or seitan.

Coriander. You can use coriander seeds whole or ground. The spice has a fresh flavor that fully releases in curries and other Asian dishes.

Cumin, a yellow-brown oblong seed with ridges, has been known and widely used in cooking in Mediterranean and Asian cuisine since ancient times. Used in savory dishes, it has a lot of health benefits and allows you create a huge variety of healthy dishes from eggplant burgers, Indian saag dip, falafel tacos to gnocchi soup.

Ginger. Fresh ground ginger is added to countless dishes. It's as common for Asian cuisine as salt or black pepper is for any cuisine. It used both for savory and sweet food. It's better to use fresh ginger, grounded by yourself.

Turmeric is a spice with a bright yellow-orange color. It is often mixed with other spices and flavors, and creates a great mustardy note in curry dishes. It's very rich in health benefits as a medicine for inflammation, Alzheimer's disease, pain, cancer, and liver damage.

Cardamom comes from South India. Several types of cardamom exist, such as green, black, and brown cardamom.

Fenugreek. This spice is commonly used for curry pastes in South India. You need to have this spice in your pantry if you want to enjoy South Indian traditional food.

Black Pepper. Peppercorns or dried fruits are ground into a powder that is known as black pepper.

Cinnamon. Another popular spice that is used both for savory and sweet food. It gives a distinctive flavor and fragrance to Asian dishes and drinks.

Saffron. The brighter color means a stronger aroma. This expensive spice will be the main secret ingredient of any Asian dish that fills your rice, meat, fish, and other meals with fragrance and makes the color of it brighter.

Sauces

Soy sauce. Of course, it is the most popular sauce in Asia. This sauce must be in your pantry anyway because no dish goes without in Asian cooking. A few variations of it exist: light, dark and thick soy sauce.

Light soy sauce is thin and salty with a light brown color. It is used for marinating, stir-fry, and dressings. Depending on the manufacturers, it can be salty with a deeper taste.

Dark soy sauce is thicker, sweeter and darker than light soy sauce. The sauce will give a beautiful caramel color to your ingredients and add to it a little bit of sweetness.

Thick soy sauce is similar to oyster sauce in some ways and is perfect for stir-fry and dips. You can also use it for stews and braised pork rice.

Teriyaki sauce consists of soy sauce and honey. Its texture is thick, even tangy. In Asian cooking it's commonly used for caramelizing meat and fish during roasting or browning.

Oyster sauce has bright taste. It's something between a salty, sweet, and earthy taste. It is used in Vietnam and Thailand.

Fish sauce has the smell of cured anchovies. It is an essential sauce used in authentic Asian recipes of ramen, broth, and home-made sauces. It makes the taste of ingredients saltier and deeper.

Chili Garlic Sauce is one of the Asian sauces that makes your dish spicier in the Asian way. Goes well with different traditional soups and stews. Also, it can be easily found in the food-store.

Gochujang. It exists in two variations: sauce and paste. This Korean paste is used for most kimchi recipes and has a spicy, slightly sweet and sour taste.

Hoisin Sauce. It is an Asian version of a BBQ sauce that has its unique flavor profile. Hoisin sauce is pretty good for marinating, topping, and glazing of dishes.

Black Bean Sauce. Another Asian sauce that includes garlic and sugar. Sweet and savory, it's commonly used for stir-fry cooking. It isn't popular abroad, so it can be a nice secret ingredient to impress somebody with a nice new taste.

Curry Paste. It is the main base ingredient for curry in any Asian region. You will only get an authentic taste of a traditional curry with this paste. It's also good for sauces, marinades, and salad dressings. The spiciness of curry paste can vary so you need to choose your preferable range of it.

CHAPTER 3. Recipes

SAUCES AND SPICES

Thai Sweet Chili Sauce

Prep time: 10 minutes

Cooking time: 20 minutes

Servings: 1

NUTRIENTS PER SERVING:

Carbohydrates – 15 g

Fat – 0 g

Protein – 0 g

Calories – 60

INGREDIENTS:

- 3 garlic cloves, peeled
- 2 hot Thai or cayenne red peppers
- ½ cup sugar
- ¾ cup water
- ¼ cup vinegar
- 1 Tbsp cornstarch
- 2 Tbsp water sliced
- ½ tsp salt

INSTRUCTIONS:

1. Set to Sauté.
2. Heat and combine all ingredients.
3. Cook until it gets thick enough.
4. Enjoy!

Ginger Sauce

Prep time: 10 minutes

Cooking time: 35 minutes

Servings: 6

NUTRIENTS PER SERVING:

Carbohydrates – 1 g

Fat – 7 g

Protein – 0 g

Calories – 64

INGREDIENTS:

- 1 yellow onion
- 2 Tbsp peeled and grated fresh ginger
- ¼ cup fresh lemon juice
- ½ cup white vinegar
- 1 cup soy sauce

INSTRUCTIONS:

1. Set to Sauté.
2. Heat and combine all ingredients.
3. Cook until it gets thick enough.
4. Enjoy!

Teriyaki Sauce

Prep time: 25 minutes

Cooking time: 40 minutes

Servings: 5

NUTRIENTS PER SERVING:

Carbohydrates – 6 g

Fat – 0 g

Protein – 2 g

Calories – 32

INGREDIENTS:

- 1 cup soy sauce
- ½ cup brown sugar
- 2 garlic cloves, minced

INSTRUCTIONS:

1. Set to Sauté.
2. Heat and combine all ingredients.
3. Cook until it gets thick enough.
4. Enjoy!

Hoisin Sauce

Prep time: 15 minutes

Cooking time: 1 hour 30 minutes

Servings: 8

NUTRIENTS PER SERVING:

Carbohydrates – 9 g

Fat – 1 g

Protein – 1 g

Calories – 40

INGREDIENTS:

- 4 Tbsp soy sauce
- 1 Tbsp black bean paste
- 1 Tbsp honey
- 2 tsp white vinegar
- ⅛ tsp garlic powder
- ⅛ tsp onion powder
- 2 tsp sesame oil
- 20 drops Chinese hot sauce
- ⅛ tsp black pepper cinnamon

INSTRUCTIONS:

1. Mix and combine all the ingredients.
2. Cook until it gets thick enough.
3. Enjoy!

Chinese Lemon Sauce

Prep time: 10 minutes

Cooking time: 20 minutes

Servings: 4

NUTRIENTS PER SERVING:

Carbohydrates – 21 g

Fat – 0 g

Protein – 0 g

Calories – 83

INGREDIENTS:

- ¼ cup sugar
- ⅓ cup chicken broth
- 1 tsp grated lemon peel
- 3 Tbsp lemon juice
- 2 Tbsp light corn syrup
- 2 Tbsp rice vinegar
- ¼ tsp salt
- 1 garlic clove, minced
- 2 tsp cornstarch
- 1 tsp cold water taste

INSTRUCTIONS:

1. Wash and mix all the ingredients.
2. Cook until it gets thick enough.
3. Enjoy!

Gochujang – Korean Red Chili Sauce

Prep time: 6 hours

Cooking time: 6 hours

Servings: 4

NUTRIENTS PER SERVING:

Carbohydrates – 14 g

Fat – 0 g

Protein – 1 g

Calories – 56

INGREDIENTS:

- 3.3 lb red chili powder
- 1.1 lb. fermented soybean powder
- 2.2 lb sweet rice powder
- 1.65 lb. milled malt barley
- 1.65 lb sea salt
- 2.2 lb rice syrup
- 5.2-quart liter water

INSTRUCTIONS:

1. Soak the malt barley in 5 liters of cold water for 5 hrs.
2. Soak the rice in water for 3-4 hours.
3. Strain the rice and remove all excess water.
4. Grind the rice in a blender. Set aside.
5. Strain the malt barley to get the liquid and white sediment.
6. Add sweet rice powder to the malt barley liquid.
7. Set to 5 hours of 60°C (140°F) on Manual.
8. Press Cancel and Set to Sauté (Normal).
9. Reduce the liquid by 20%. Then cool it down.
10. Add the soybean, rice powder and sea salt.
11. Add rice syrup to taste.
12. Mix everything thoroughly.
13. Transfer the sauce into the clay pot.
14. Sprinkle with a pinch of sea salt.
15. Enjoy!

Chinese 5 Spice Mix

Prep time: 10 minutes

Cooking time: 10 minutes

Servings: 10

NUTRIENTS PER SERVING:

Carbohydrates – 4 g

Fat – 0 g

Protein – 0 g

Calories – 21

INGREDIENTS:

- 2 tsp star anise
- 1 tsp fennel seeds
- 2 tsp Sichuan peppercorns
- 1 tsp ginger
- 2 tsp cinnamon

INSTRUCTIONS:

1. Add all the ingredients to a blender.
2. Make a smooth powder.
3. Place in a glass jar.
4. Enjoy!

Garam Masala

Prep time: 5 minutes

Cooking time: none

Servings: 8

NUTRIENTS PER SERVING:

Carbohydrates – 0.8 g

Fat – 0.2 g

Protein – 0.2 g

Calories – 4.6

INGREDIENTS:

- ½ cup coriander seeds
- 1 Tbsp fennel seeds
- 4 stars anise
- ½ Tbsp cloves
- 1 Tbsp black pepper
- ½ Tbsp jeera
- 2 cardamom
- 6 cardamom
- 3 sticks cinnamon

INSTRUCTIONS:

1. Add all the ingredients to a blender.
2. Make a smooth powder.
3. Place in a glass jar.
4. Enjoy!

Chai Spice Mix

Prep time: 10 minutes

Cooking time: 5 minutes

Servings: 8

NUTRIENTS PER SERVING:

Carbohydrates – 1.4 g

Fat – 0.1 g

Protein – 0.2 g

Calories – 7

INGREDIENTS:

- 3 Tbsp green cardamom pods
- 1 Tbsp whole black peppercorns
- 2½ cinnamon sticks
- 1 star anise
- 2 Tbsp whole mace
- 10 whole cloves
- ½ whole nutmeg, grated
- 2 Tbsp ground ginger

INSTRUCTIONS:

1. Set to Sauté (Low).
2. Heat all the spices and dry for 3 minutes.
3. Let the spice mix cool down.
4. Grind into a fine powder.
5. Add in the nutmeg and ground ginger.
6. Enjoy!

Curry Powder

Prep time: 5 minutes

Cooking time: 5 minutes

Servings: 5

NUTRIENTS PER SERVING:

Carbohydrates – 5 g

Fat – 1 g

Protein – 1 g

Calories – 25

INGREDIENTS:

- 2 Tbsp coriander, ground
- 2 Tbsp cumin, ground
- 1½ Tbsp turmeric, ground
- 2 tsp ginger, ground
- 1 tsp dry mustard
- ½ tsp black pepper, ground
- 1 tsp cinnamon, ground
- ½ tsp cardamom, ground
- ½ tsp cayenne pepper

INSTRUCTIONS:

1. Combine spices in a small jar.
2. Shake it well.
3. Enjoy!

BREAKFAST

Eight Treasure Congee

Prep time: 10 hours

Cooking time: 45 minutes

Servings: 4

NUTRIENTS PER SERVING:

Carbohydrates – 33 g

Fat – 2 g

Protein – 4 g

Calories – 172

INGREDIENTS:

- ½ cup glutinous rice, soaked for 1 hour
- 2 Tbsp black rice
- 1 Tbsp peanuts
- 5 Chinese dried red dates
- 1 Tbsp mung beans, soaked for 4 hours
- 1 Tbsp red beans
- 1 Tbsp corn flakes
- 10 dried Longan
- ½ Tbsp walnut
- 6 cups water

INSTRUCTIONS:

1. Add all the ingredients to the pot.
2. Pour in around 6 cups of water.
3. Lock the lid. Turn the valve to Sealing.
4. Set to 30 minutes of Beans.
5. Do a natural release.
6. Serve warm.

Nikujaga – Japanese Stewed Beef and Potatoes

Prep time: 15 minutes

Cooking time: 30 minutes

Servings: 4

NUTRIENTS PER SERVING:

Carbohydrates – 20 g

Fat – 7g

Protein – 6 g

Calories – 170

INGREDIENTS:

- 10 green beans, cut in half
- 1 onion, cut in half
- 1 carrot, peeled and cut into rolling wedges
- 2 potatoes, cut into quarters and soaked
- 1 package shirataki noodles, drained and cut into thirds
- ½ lb. thinly sliced beef, cut into small pieces
- 1 Tbsp oil
- 1 pinch salt
- 1 Tbsp sugar
- 1 cup dashi
- 3 Tbsp mirin
- 2 Tbsp sake
- 3 Tbsp soy sauce

INSTRUCTIONS:

1. Blanch the green beans in boiling water until tender. Drain and set aside.
2. Set to Sauté and heat the oil.
3. Add the onion. Cook for 2-3 minutes.
4. Add the meat and mix well.
5. Add the potatoes, carrots and shirataki noodles.
6. Add the sugar, dashi, mirin, sake and soy sauce.
7. Lock the lid. Turn the valve to Sealing.
8. Set to 15 minutes of Meat/Stew.
9. Do a natural release.
10. Add the green beans to heat them up.
11. Serve hot.

Congee with Bacon and Egg

Prep time: 5 minutes

Cooking time: 35 minutes

Servings: 6

NUTRIENTS PER SERVING:

Carbohydrates – 28 g

Fat – 37 g

Protein – 18 g

Calories – 525

INGREDIENTS:

- 1 cup white rice uncooked
- 8 cups water
- 8 oz bacon uncooked
- 2-inch ginger, peeled and bruised
- 4 cloves garlic, peeled and smashed
- 2 scallions, chopped
- Salt to taste
- Soy sauce, to taste
- Sriracha to taste
- 6 scallions diced
- 12 slices bacon cooked
- 6 eggs soft-boiled

INSTRUCTIONS:

1. Add the rice, water, uncooked bacon, ginger, garlic, and whole scallions to the pot.
2. Set to 30 minutes of high pressure.
3. Do a natural release.
4. Remove the bacon.
5. Add salt and soy/fish sauces to taste.
6. Set to Sauté and cook for 5 minutes.
7. Serve with l crumbled rasher of bacon, a soft-boiled egg, and scallions.

Quinoa Breakfast Bowl

Prep time: 25 minutes

Cooking time: 1 minute

Servings: 6

NUTRIENTS PER SERVING:

Carbohydrates – 36 g

Fat – 2 g

Protein – 6 g

Calories – 197

INGREDIENTS:

- ½ cups quinoa, soaked for 1 hour and drained
- 1 can coconut milk
- 1½ cups water
- 1 teaspoon ground cinnamon
- ¼ cup pure maple syrup
- 2 teaspoons vanilla extract
- ¼ teaspoon salt
- Fresh fruit for topping
- Coconut flakes for topping
- Non-dairy milk for topping

INSTRUCTIONS:

1. Add the quinoa, coconut milk, water, cinnamon, maple syrup, vanilla and salt to the pot.
2. Lock the lid. Turn the valve to Sealing.
3. Set to 12 minutes of Rice.
4. Do a natural release.
5. Serve with milk, fresh fruit, coconut flakes, or any other toppings you like.

Takikomi Gohan – Japanese Mixed Rice

Prep time: 35 minutes
Cooking time: 35 minutes
Servings: 4

NUTRIENTS PER SERVING:

Carbohydrates – 70 g
Fat – 4 g
Protein – 10 g
Calories – 365

INGREDIENTS:

- 2 rice measuring cups uncooked Japanese short grain rice
- 2 dried shiitake mushrooms, sliced
- 2 Tbsp of reserved liquid from hydrating shiitake mushrooms
- ¼ cup water
- 1 chicken thigh, marinated in sake
- ½ Tbsp sake
- 1.8 oz gobo, thinly sliced and soaked
- 1.8 oz carrot, sliced
- 1 piece deep fried tofu pouch, sliced and squeezed
- A pinch of green onion, chopped
- 1½ cup dashi
- 1½ Tbsp soy sauce
- 1 Tbsp mirin
- ½ tsp kosher salt

INSTRUCTIONS:

1. In a bowl add ¼ cup water to dried shiitake. Submerge the mushrooms under the water with a heavy object.
2. Squeeze the shiitake into the bowl. Remove the stem from each mushroom.
3. Mix the reserved liquid from hydrating shiitake mushrooms, soy sauce, mirin, salt, and dashi in a cup.
4. Combine the gobo, chicken, tofu, mushrooms, carrot, and previous step seasonings.
5. Put the rice into the pot and place the ingredients and liquids over the rice. DO NOT MIX.
6. Lock the lid. Turn the valve to Sealing.
7. Set to 2 minutes of high pressure.
8. Do a natural release.
9. Fluff the rice with a rice scooper.
10. Serve with chopped green onion.

Black Rice Pudding

Prep time: 5 minutes

Cooking time: 45 minutes

Servings: 4

NUTRIENTS PER SERVING:

Carbohydrates - 38 g

Fat – 19 g

Protein – 5 g

Calories – 338

INGREDIENTS:

- 1 cup black rice, rinsed and drained
- 1 cup Water
- ½ cups Full-Fat Coconut Milk
- ½ cup sugar
- ½ tsp Salt
- 1 cup full-fat coconut milk

INSTRUCTIONS:

1. Add all of the ingredients (except 1 cup coconut milk) to the pot.
2. Set to 22 minutes of high pressure.
3. Do a natural and quick-release.
4. Stir well to break up the rice grains.
5. Gradually pour in 1 cup of coconut milk while stirring.
6. Let it sit for 5-10 minutes.
7. Serve and enjoy!

Chawanmushi – Steamed Egg Custard

Prep time: 20 minutes
Cooking time: 20 minutes
Servings: 5

NUTRIENTS PER SERVING:

Carbohydrates – 4 g
Fat – 7 g
Protein – 13 g
Calories – 137

INGREDIENTS:

- 1¾ cup dashi
- 3 large eggs
- 1 tsp mirin
- 1 tsp light-color soy sauce
- ½ tsp salt
- 1 chicken thigh, cut into bite-sized pieces
- 5 shrimp
- 2 Tbsp sake
- 1.4 oz carrot, cut into ¼ inch slices
- 5 stalks mitsuba
- 2.3 oz shimeji mushrooms, cut
- 1-inch Kamaboko, sliced

INSTRUCTIONS:

1. Place the chicken and shrimp in different bowls and add 1 Tbsp sake to each.
2. Make a knot with the mitsuba stem.
3. Break the eggs in a large bowl whisk them.

4. Add dashi, mirin, soy sauce, and ½ tsp kosher salt. Whisk well.
5. Strain the egg mixture.
6. Place the ingredients in a ramekin.
7. Cover the cups with a sheet of foil.
8. Pour in 1 cup of water into the pot. Place the steamer rack inside.
9. Put the cups in steamer rack.
10. Lock the lid. Turn the valve to Sealing.
11. Set to 0 minutes of Steam (low pressure).
12. Do a natural release for 15 minutes.
13. Take out 1 cup to check if it is done.
14. If the egg custard isn't fully cooked (liquid comes out), repeat the steam process, and do a quick-release.
15. Serve hot with a small spoon.

Mushroom Ramekin Eggs

Prep time: 10 minutes

Cooking time: 10 minutes

Servings: 4

NUTRIENTS PER SERVING:

Carbohydrates – 6 g

Fat – 9 g

Protein – 14 g

Calories – 150

INGREDIENTS:

- 1 Tbsp ghee for greasing
- 2 cups mushrooms, chopped
- 2 cups of water
- 1 Tbsp chives, chopped
- 3 eggs
- 3 Tbsp heavy cream
- Salt to taste

INSTRUCTIONS:

1. Set to Sauté and melt the ghee.
2. Add the mushrooms and cook until tender. Add salt to taste.
3. Grease the ramekins. Divide the mushrooms into the ramekins.
4. Add 1 tsp of chives, a freshly cracked egg, 1 Tbsp of cream to each ramekin.
5. Pour water into the bottom of the pot.
6. Put in the trivet, and put the ramekins on top.
7. Lock the lid and set to 2 minutes of low pressure.
8. Do a quick-release.
9. Serve with toast.

Miso Oatmeal

Prep time: 5 minutes

Cooking time: 8 minutes

Servings: 2

NUTRIENTS PER SERVING:

Carbohydrates – 32 g

Fat – 11 g

Protein – 13 g

Calories – 281

INGREDIENTS:

- 1½ cup steel-cut oats uncooked
- 1 cup unsweetened almond milk
- 1 cup water
- 1 cup frozen kale, chopped
- 1 Tbsp miso paste
- 4 Tbsp nutritional yeast
- 1 tsp tamari
- 1 Tbsp tahini
- ½ avocado, diced
- 2 green onions, sliced

INSTRUCTIONS:

1. Add the steel cut oats, water, and almond milk to the pot.
2. Set to 8 minutes of Porridge.
3. Do a natural release.
4. Optional:
5. Set to sauté, stir in the kale, miso paste, tahini, tamari, and nutritional yeast.
6. Cook, stirring for 2-3 minutes to heat up the frozen kale.
7. Serve with avocado and green onions.
8. Enjoy!

Pork Pho with Bacon

Prep time: 5 minutes
Cooking time: 1 hour
Servings: 4

NUTRIENTS PER SERVING:

Carbohydrates – 111 g
Fat – 30 g
Protein – 19 g
Calories – 802

INGREDIENTS:

- 2 star anise
- 8-10 whole cloves
- 1 cinnamon stick
- 1 onion, quartered
- 2" knob ginger peeled, cut into chunks
- 3 lb pork bones
- 3 slices bacon
- 1 Fuji apple, cored and diced
- 2 tsp salt
- 2 pieces Chinese yellow rock sugar
- 2 Tbsp fish sauce
- 8 slices bacon, cooked to taste
- 4 eggs, hard boil
- 1 lb Banh Pho rice noodles
- 1 tsp sesame oil

INSTRUCTIONS:

1. Set to sauté and add the star anise, cloves, cinnamon to the pot.
2. Cook for 3-4 minutes, stirring occasionally.
3. Add the onion and ginger. Cook for 1 minute.
4. Add pork bones, bacon and 2 cups of water.
5. Add the apple and salt. Pour in water up to the max fill line.
6. Let it boil then lock the lid.
7. Set to 30 minutes of pressure cook.
8. Do a natural release.
9. Strain into a large pot.
10. Cook the broth over a medium heat, adding the rock sugar and fish sauce.
11. Cook the rice noodles following package directions.
12. Rinse noodles and add the sesame oil. Toss well.
13. Put ¼ of the noodles into a bowl, Crumble in 2 slices bacon, add the halved egg and hot broth.
14. Serve hot.

SOUPS ANS STEWS

Ramen Soup

Prep time: 25 minutes

Cooking time: 20 minutes

Servings: 6

NUTRIENTS PER SERVING:

Carbohydrates – 27 g

Fat – 28 g

Protein –30 g

Calories – 478

INGREDIENTS:

- ½ Tbsp of sesame oil
- 1 tsp grated ginger
- 3 cloves of garlic, minced
- 8 oz fresh mushrooms, sliced
- 3-4 pound chicken, giblets removed and discarded
- 2 Tbsp soy sauce
- 8 cups water
- Salt and pepper
- 8 ounces udon noodles
- A pinch of green onion, chopped
- Soft boiled eggs for garnish (optional)
- Sesame seeds for garnish

INSTRUCTIONS:

1. Set to sauté (Normal) and heat the sesame oil.
2. Add the garlic and ginger. Cook for 1-2 minutes.
3. Add the mushrooms, water, soy sauce, salt, pepper, and chicken to the pot.
4. Press Cancel, lock and set the vent to Sealing.
5. Set to 20 minutes of high pressure.
6. Do a quick-release.
7. Take out the chicken. Set aside.
8. Set to sauté and bring the chicken broth to boil.
9. Add the noodles (cook following package directions).
10. Meanwhile, shred the chicken and discard the bones and skin.
11. When the noodles are done, add the chicken.
12. Serve with chopped green onion, soft boiled egg and sesame seeds.
13. Enjoy!

Pork Belly Ramen

Prep time: 15 minutes
Cooking time: 45 minutes
Servings: 2

NUTRIENTS PER SERVING:

Carbohydrates – 45 g
Fat – 28 g
Protein – 40 g
Calories – 700

INGREDIENTS:

- 1 pound pork belly
- 1 tsp salt
- ½ cup white onions, chopped
- 2 cloves garlic, crushed
- 1 Tbsp ginger, minced
- 1 1oz package dried shiitake mushrooms
- 4 cups beef broth
- 2 Tbsp dark soy sauce
- 2 Tbsp dark brown sugar
- 2 cups water
- 1 package Ramen Noodles
- ¼ cup green onions, chopped
- 2 soft boiled eggs
- Oil

INSTRUCTIONS:

1. Dry the pork belly with a paper towel and season with salt.
2. Set to Sauté (High) and brown one side for 3-4 minutes.
3. Add the onion and flip the meat to brown the other side.
4. Add garlic and ginger, and sauté for 2 minutes. Turn off.
5. Add the dried shitake mushrooms and pour in the broth.
6. Lock the lid and set the vent to Sealing.
7. Set to 25 minutes of high pressure.
8. Do a natural release.
9. Take out the pork belly and put on a chopping board.
10. Pour the rest of the broth into a bowl.
11. Set to Sauté (High) and slice the pork belly.
12. Sauté the slices, soy sauce, and brown sugar.
13. Slowly flip the slices to coat with sugar mixture for 3-4 minutes. Set aside.
14. Add water to the pot to stop the sugar burning.
15. Pour the broth into the pot and let it boil.
16. Add the noodles and cook for 3 minutes.
17. Serve with chopped green onions and soft-boiled eggs.

Miso Soup

Prep time: 10 minutes

Cooking time: 15 minutes

Servings: 4

NUTRIENTS PER SERVING:

Carbohydrates – 12 g

Fat – 12 g

Protein – 26 g

Calories – 170

INGREDIENTS:

- 2 Tbsp oil
- 1 onion, diced
- 2 cloves garlic, diced
- 1-inch piece ginger, peeled and minced
- 2 cups mushrooms, sliced
- 2 cups kale, chopped
- 4 cups vegetable broth
- 1 Tbsp miso paste
- 14 ounces firm tofu flakes, cut into cubes

INSTRUCTIONS:

1. Add the oil, onion, garlic, ginger, and mushrooms to the pot.
2. Set to Sauté and cook for 5 minutes, stirring.
3. Add chopped kale and cook for 2 minutes.
4. Add the broth and miso paste. Mix well.
5. Lock the lid. Turn the valve to Sealing.
6. Set to 3 minutes of high pressure.
7. Do a natural release.
8. Add the tofu cubes to the soup.
9. Set to Sauté and let the soup boil.
10. Cook for 5 minutes and then serve.

Kimchi Jjigae

Prep time: 10 minutes

Cooking time: 20 minutes

Servings: 4

NUTRIENTS PER SERVING:

Carbohydrates – 49 g

Fat – 14 g

Protein – 17 g

Calories – 379

INGREDIENTS:

- 1-½ pounds kimchi, cut into bite-size pieces
- 8 ounces fatty pork or beef, cut into bite size pieces
- 1 Tbsp sesame oil
- 1 to 3 tsp red chili pepper flakes
- ½ cup kimchi juice
- 2 cups of water
- 1 Tbsp soup soy sauce
- 1 Tbsp garlic, minced
- 8 ounces tofu, sliced
- 2 scallions, chopped
- Black pepper to taste
- 1 to 2 tsp of sugar (optional)

INSTRUCTIONS:

1. Set to Sauté and add the meat, kimchi, sesame oil, and red pepper flakes.
2. Cook until the meat until it's done (5 minutes).
3. Add the kimchi juice, water, soup soy sauce, and garlic.
4. Lock the lid. Turn the valve to Sealing.
5. Set to 10 minutes of Soup mode.
6. Do a quick release.
7. Add the tofu and scallions to the pot.
8. Set to Sauté and boil the kimchi to the desired tenderness.
9. Enjoy!

Shrimp Tom Kha

Prep time: 15 minutes

Cooking time: 10 minutes

Servings: 4

NUTRIENTS PER SERVING:

Carbohydrates – 5 g

Fat – 14 g

Protein – 13 g

Calories – 185

INGREDIENTS:

- 3 cups chicken broth or water
- ½ pound shrimp, peeled (tails left on) and deveined
- 1 cup canned straw mushrooms, undrained
- 1 can full-fat coconut milk
- 6 to 8 thin slices fresh ginger
- 2 Tbsp fish sauce
- 1 Tbsp lemongrass, minced
- 1 tsp honey
- ½ tsp salt
- Grated zest of 1 lime
- ¼ cup fresh lime juice
- A pinch of cilantro, chopped

INSTRUCTIONS:

1. Add the broth, shrimp, mushrooms and their liquid, half the coconut milk, the ginger, 1 Tbsp of fish sauce, lemongrass, honey and salt to the inner pot.
2. Lock the lid. Turn the valve to Sealing.
3. Set to 1 minute of low pressure.
4. Do a quick release.
5. Add the rest of fish sauce, coconut milk, lime zest and lime juice.
6. Serve with chopped cilantro.
7. Enjoy!

Bak Kut Teh – Pork Ribs Soup

Prep time: 10 minutes

Cooking time: 50 minutes

Servings: 6

NUTRIENTS PER SERVING:

Carbohydrates – 10 g

Fat – 37 g

Protein – 28 g

Calories – 487

INGREDIENTS:

- 2 lbs pork ribs
- 4 cups water
- 4 cups pork broth
- 1 Tbsp black pepper
- 1 Tbsp white pepper
- 2 whole star anise
- 10 garlic cloves peeled
- 1 Tbsp dark soy sauce
- 1 Tbsp palm sugar
- 1 Tbsp oyster sauce
- 10 dried shiitake, soaked and halved
- 10 red Thai chilies, sliced
- Salt to taste
- 1 bunch green onions, cut into pieces
- 6 oz. fried tofu, cubed

INSTRUCTIONS:

1. Prepare the ribs: clean membranes from the back of the ribs.
2. Cut them into individual ribs.
3. Boil the ribs in a pot for 10-15 minute. Drain the ribs.
4. Add all the ingredients to the pot (except tofu, green onion, Thai chilies).
5. Set to 45 minutes of high pressure.
6. Do a quick-release.
7. Set to Sauté and let it simmer.
8. Add the green onion, tofu, and cook for 3 minutes.
9. Serve with rice and Thai chilies.

Laksa Soup

Prep time: 10 minutes
Cooking time: 30 minutes
Servings: 4

NUTRIENTS PER SERVING:

Carbohydrates – 64 g
Fat – 31 g
Protein – 23 g
Calories – 613

INGREDIENTS:

- 2 Tbsp dried shrimp, soaked for 15 minutes
- 3 dried red chilies, soaked for 15 minutes
- 1 Tbsp kashmiri red chili powder
- 1 and ½ tsp freshly ground coriander
- 1 Tbsp finely chopped lemongrass
- 1 tsp ground turmeric
- 2 shallots quartered
- 5 cloves of garlic peeled
- 1 large 1-inch piece fresh ginger
- 2 Tbsp fish sauce
- 3 Tbsp oil
- 3 chicken thighs, skinned and bone
- 3 cups water
- 2 carrots, thinly sliced
- 1 bell pepper, thinly sliced
- 1 can of coconut milk
- 2 to 3 ounces thin rice vermicelli
- 2 Tbsp fresh lime juice
- Chopped basil and cilantro

INSTRUCTIONS:

1. Add the dried shrimp, chilies, coriander, kashmiri red chili powder, shallots, turmeric, garlic, ginger, and fish sauce to the food processor and mince.
2. Set to Sauté and heat the oil.
3. Add the spice paste and cook for 1 minute.
4. Add the chicken and pour in the water.
5. Press Cancel and mix well.
6. Set to 5 minutes of high pressure.
7. Do a quick-release.
8. Take out the meat and cut it into shreds.
9. Take the bones out the pot.
10. Add the carrot, bell pepper, coconut milk, water and vermicelli.
11. Lock the lid.
12. Set to 1 minute of low pressure.
13. Do a quick-release.
14. Squeeze in the lime juice and add chopped greens. Enjoy!

Galbitang – Short Ribs Soup

Prep time: 35 minutes

Cooking time: 30 minutes

Servings: 6

NUTRIENTS PER SERVING:

Carbohydrates – 6 g

Fat – 10 g

Protein – 19 g

Calories – 198

INGREDIENTS:

- 1.5 lb beef short ribs
- 8 cups water
- 1 yellow onion with skin on
- 2 green onions for cooking broth
- 2 green onions, chopped
- 2 thick slices of ginger
- ½ Korean radish, cut into chunks
- 2 Tbsp garlic, chopped
- 2 tsp guk ganjang
- 1 tsp salt

INSTRUCTIONS:

1. Trim off the excess fat from the meat.
2. Soak the ribs in cold water for an hour to draw out the blood.

3. Add in the green onions, ribs, radish, whole yellow onion and ginger. Pour in the water.
4. Lock the lid and set the vent to Sealing.
5. Set to 30 minutes of Soup.
6. Do a quick-release.
7. Skim off the fat from the soup.
8. Season with guk ganjang, salt, garlic. Enjoy!

Miyeok Guk – Seaweed Soup

Prep time: 5 minutes

Cooking time: 25 minutes

Servings: 6

NUTRIENTS PER SERVING:

Carbohydrates – 5 g

Fat – 4 g

Protein – 6 g

Calories – 88

INGREDIENTS:

- 50g dried seaweed, soaked and cut into bite-sized chunks
- 1 lb beef, cut into pieces
- 1 Tbsp sesame oil
- 4 cloves garlic, minced
- 12 cups water
- 2-3 Tbsp soup soy sauce
- Salt to taste

INSTRUCTIONS:

1. Set to Sauté and heat the oil.
2. Add the beef and brown it.
3. Add the seaweed and garlic. Mix well.
4. Pour in the water and soy sauce.
5. Lock the lid. Turn the valve to Sealing.
6. Set to 15 minutes of Meat/Stew.
7. Do a quick-release.
8. Add salt to taste.
9. Enjoy!

Chinese Pork Shoulder Soup

Prep time: 15 minutes

Cooking time: 1 hour 15 minutes

Servings: 6

NUTRIENTS PER SERVING:

Carbohydrates – 37 g

Fat – 16 g

Protein – 37 g

Calories – 447

INGREDIENTS:

- 1 tsp Chinese Five Spice
- ½ tsp crushed red pepper
- 1 cup dark soy sauce
- 8 cloves garlic, peeled
- ¼ cup dark brown sugar, packed
- 5 cups chicken broth
- 1 tsp kosher salt
- 2 Tbsp sesame oil
- 4 green onions, chopped
- 2 inches fresh ginger, unpeeled and sliced
- 8 dried shiitake mushrooms
- 3 lbs pork shoulder, trimmed
- 1 lb baby bok choy bottom, chopped
- 6 oz fine egg noodles

INSTRUCTIONS:

1. Add all of the spices, the sesame oil, soy sauce, chicken broth, brown sugar, garlic, green onions, and ginger slices into the pot. Mix well.
2. Add the pork to the pot.
3. Lock the lid and set the vent to Sealing.
4. Set to 45 minutes of high pressure.
5. When the cooking is almost done, cook the egg noodles, following the package directions.
6. Do a quick-release.
7. Remove the mushrooms, ginger and garlic.
8. Slice the mushrooms and put back in the pot.
9. Add the baby bok choy.
10. Lock the lid and set to 1 minute of high pressure.
11. Do a quick-release.
12. Stir noodles into the soup.
13. Serve hot. Enjoy!

CHICKEN

Teriyaki Chicken

Prep time: 10 minutes

Cooking time: 20 minutes

Servings: 4

NUTRIENTS PER SERVING:

Carbohydrates – 24 g

Fat – 6 g

Protein – 50 g

Calories – 360

INGREDIENTS:

- 2 pounds chicken breast, boneless and skinless
- 1¾ cups water
- ⅔ cup soy sauce
- ¾ cup honey
- 2 Tbsp rice vinegar
- 2 Tbsp mirin rice wine, optional
- 1 Tbsp minced garlic,
- 2 tsp minced ginger,
- 3 Tbsp cornstarch,
- 2 Tbsp green onion, thinly sliced

INSTRUCTIONS:

1. Put the chicken into the pot.
2. Combine the soy sauce, rice vinegar, 1½ cups of water, rice wine, honey, garlic, and ginger in a bowl.
3. Pour the teriyaki sauce into the pot.
4. Lock the lid. Turn the valve to Sealing.
5. Set to 10 minutes of high pressure.
6. Do a quick-release.
7. Take out the chicken and transfer to a clean plate.
8. Let it rest for 5-10 minutes before slicing.
9. To make a slurry mix the cornstarch and a ¼ cup of water.
10. Set to Sauté and let the teriyaki sauce simmer.
11. Stir in the cornstarch slurry gradually, while mixing (1-2 minutes).
12. Turn off when the desired thickness is achieved.
13. Serve with chopped green onion.

Teriyaki Wings

Prep time: 5 minutes
Cooking time: 35 minutes
Servings: 6

NUTRIENTS PER SERVING:

Carbohydrates – 8 g
Fat – 33 g
Protein – 35 g
Calories –479

INGREDIENTS:

- ½ cup soy sauce
- ⅓ cup sugar
- ½ tsp black pepper
- 1 tsp Sriracha sauce
- 2 Tbsp garlic, minced
- 2 Tbsp ginger, minced
- 1 tsp sesame oil
- 2 Tbsp rice vinegar
- ¼ tsp cinnamon powder
- 2½ lbs chicken wings
- 1 Tbsp vegetable oil
- 1 Tbsp cornstarch
- 1 Tbsp water
- 1 to 2 tsp sesame seeds, toasted
- 2 Tbsp green onions, thinly sliced
- A pinch of cilantro, chopped

INSTRUCTIONS:

1. Mix the soy sauce, sugar, pepper, sriracha, garlic, sesame oil, ginger, rice wine vinegar, and cinnamon in the pot.
2. Add the chicken wings to the pot and coat them with sauce.
3. Lock the lid and set to 5 minutes of high pressure.
4. Line a baking sheet with foil, add the vegetable oil.
5. Do a natural release.
6. Take out the wings and put onto a baking sheet.
7. Set to Sauté and let the sauce simmer.
8. Gradually stir cornstarch and water together to make a paste, stirring to get the desired thickness. Press Cancel.
9. To caramelize the wings place them onto the baking sheet and baste with sauce.
10. Place them into the broiler and cook for 15 minutes. Flip the wings after 7 minutes.
11. Serve with green onion, sesame seeds, and teriyaki sauce.

Cashew Chicken

Prep time: 15 minutes

Cooking time: 15 minutes

Servings: 4

NUTRIENTS PER SERVING:

Carbohydrates – 13 g

Fat – 15 g

Protein – 49 g

Calories – 380

INGREDIENTS:

- 2 lbs boneless, skinless chicken thighs, cut into bite-size pieces
- ¼ tsp black pepper
- ¼ cup low sodium soy sauce
- 2 Tbsp rice vinegar
- 2 Tbsp ketchup
- 1 Tbsp brown sugar
- 1 garlic clove, minced
- 1 tsp ginger, minced
- ⅛ tsp ground red pepper
- 1 Tbsp cornstarch
- 1 Tbsp water
- ⅓ cup cashews
- Sliced green onions, for garnish
- Toasted sesame seeds, for garnish

INSTRUCTIONS:

1. Put the chicken into the pot.
2. Add the brown sugar, soy sauce, ginger vinegar, pepper, ketchup, garlic, and red pepper.
3. Toss to coat meat with sauce.
4. Lock the lid. Turn the valve to Sealing.
5. Set to 6 minutes of high pressure.
6. Do a natural release.
7. Mix the cornstarch and water in a bowl to make a slurry.
8. Stir in the slurry gradually into the pot.
9. Set to Sauté and let it simmer.
10. Cook for 3-4 minutes until it becomes the desired thickness.
11. Add the cashews. Serve with sliced green onions and toasted sesame seeds. Enjoy!

Tandoori Chicken

Prep time: 5 minutes
Cooking time: 15 minutes
Servings: 4-6

NUTRIENTS PER SERVING:

Carbohydrates – 8 g
Fat – 8 g
Protein – 24 g
Calories – 177

INGREDIENTS:

- ½ cup onion, chopped
- 1 Tbsp ginger, chopped
- 1 Tbsp garlic, chopped
- 1 jalapeno, chopped
- 1 Tbsp ground coriander
- 1 tsp ground cumin
- 1 tsp turmeric
- 1 tsp garam masala
- ¼ tsp black pepper
- 1 Tbsp paprika
- 1 Tbsp brown sugar
- 1 tsp salt
- ¼ tsp cayenne pepper
- 2 Tbsp lemon juice
- 1 cup yogurt
- ¼ cup chicken broth
- 6 chicken thighs, bone-in and skinless
- Vegetable oil to coat the tray

INSTRUCTIONS:

1. Add the onions, cumin, ginger, garlic, jalapeno, turmeric, garam masala, black pepper, coriander, paprika, lemon juice, brown sugar, cayenne pepper, yogurt, chicken broth, and salt to a blender to make a smooth paste.
2. Add the mixture and chicken to the pot. Mix well to cover the chicken.
3. Lock the lid. Turn the valve to Sealing.
4. Set to 15 pressure of high pressure.
5. Do a quick-release.
6. Take out the meat and set aside.
7. Set to Sauté (Low) and cook the sauce for 10 minutes to make it thicker.
8. Cover a baking tray with foil and pour on the oil. Preheat a broiler.
9. Glaze both sides of thighs with sauce.
10. Put in the broiler and cook until the chicken is grilled.
11. Serve with rice or naan.
12. Enjoy!

Mango Chicken

Prep time: 5 minutes

Cooking time: 6 minutes

Servings: 4

NUTRIENTS PER SERVING:

Carbohydrates – 29 g

Fat – 4 g

Protein – 37 g

Calories – 313

INGREDIENTS:

- 1 cup + 2 Tbsp mango juice
- 1 Tbsp ginger, minced
- 1 Tbsp garlic, minced
- 1 tsp tamari
- 1.5 Tbsp dark brown sugar
- 1.5 pounds chicken breasts, boneless and skinless, cubed
- 1 Tbsp lime juice
- 2 Tbsp cornstarch
- 2 cups fresh mango chunks
- Few cilantro leaves

INSTRUCTIONS:

1. Add the mango juice, ginger, garlic, tamari/soy sauce, and sugar to the Instant Pot insert and whisk to combine.
2. Add the chicken and stir to coat.
3. Lock the lid. Turn the valve to Sealing.
4. Set to 5 minutes of high pressure.
5. Do a quick-release.
6. Mix 2 Tbsp mango juice, lime juice and cornstarch well.
7. Set to Sauté and add in cornstarch mixture to the chicken.
8. Cook for 3-4 minutes, stirring occasionally.
9. Add the mango chunks and warm them.
10. Serve with rice and cilantro leaves.

General Tso Chicken

Prep time: 10 minutes
Cooking time: 10 minutes
Servings: 3

NUTRIENTS PER SERVING:

Carbohydrates – 15 g
Fat – 11 g
Protein – 39 g
Calories – 659

INGREDIENTS:

- 1-1.5 lbs skinless and boneless chicken thighs, cut into cubes
- 2 Tbsp canola oil
- 1 Tbsp garlic, minced
- 1 Tbsp ginger, minced
- 1 Tbsp red chili sauce
- 1 Tbsp hoisin sauce
- 1 Tbsp light soy sauce
- 2 Tbsp Chinese wine Shaoxing wine
- 2 tsp lemon juice
- 2 Tbsp brown sugar
- ⅓ cup chicken stock
- 2 tsp corn starch
- 5-6 dried red chilies
- Salt and pepper
- 1 pinch of green onion, chopped
- Toasted white sesame seeds
- Oil

INSTRUCTIONS:

1. Set to Sauté and add chicken. Cook for 1-2 minutes.
2. Add the ginger, garlic, dried red chilies, scallions, hoisin sauce, soy sauce, brown sugar, Chinese wine vinegar, lemon juice, chili sauce, salt, and pepper. Stir well.
3. Add 5-7 Tbsp chicken stock.
4. Lock the lid and set to 5 minutes of Poultry.
5. If chicken isn't done, set to Sauté and cook for a couple of minutes until the meat is smooth, then your chicken is cooked well.
6. Do a natural release.
7. Mix flour with little water.
8. Set to Sauté and stir in the mixture to make the sauce thicker. Cook for 2-3 minutes once it is simmering.
9. Serve with rice, green onions, and sesame seeds. Enjoy!

Kung Pao Chicken

Prep time: 10 minutes
Cooking time: 10 minutes
Servings: 6

NUTRIENTS PER SERVING:

Carbohydrates – 33 g
Fat – 15 g
Protein – 9 g
Calories – 300

INGREDIENTS:

- 1 Tbsp cornstarch
- ¼ tsp black pepper
- ⅛ tsp salt
- 1 lb chicken breasts, boneless skinless
- 3 Tbsp olive oil
- 1 red bell pepper, chopped
- 1 zucchini, chopped
- 1 tsp red pepper flakes
- 2 Tbsp cornstarch
- 3 Tbsp water
- ⅓ cup soy sauce
- ½ cup water
- 2 Tbsp honey
- 3 Tbsp hoisin sauce
- 3 garlic cloves, minced
- 1 tsp ginger, grated
- ¼ tsp red pepper flakes

INSTRUCTIONS:

1. Put the black pepper, cornstarch, salt, and chicken into a zip-lock bag and shake to coat. Set aside.
2. Mix the rest of the ingredients except chicken, bell pepper, zucchini, and red pepper flakes in a bowl.
3. Set to Saute and heat the oil.
4. Brown the chicken on each side for 3-4 minutes.
5. Transfer the meat to a paper towel-lined plate.
6. Put the meat back in the pot and coat with sauce.
7. Lock the lid and set the vent to Sealing
8. Set to 3 minutes of high pressure.
9. Do a natural or quick-release.
10. Take out the meat and set to Sauté.
11. Add in the bell pepper, zucchini, and red pepper flakes. Sauté for 2-3 minutes.
12. Mix cornstarch and water and stir it in to make the sauce thicker.
13. Put the meat back in the pot to heat it
14. Serve with brown rice. Enjoy!

Chicken Tikka Masala

Prep time: 30 minutes

Cooking time: 30 minutes

Servings: 6

NUTRIENTS PER SERVING:

Carbohydrates – 57 g

Fat – 17 g

Protein – 44 g

Calories – 578

INGREDIENTS:

- 2.5-3 pounds chicken breasts, cubed
- ½ cup full-fat Greek yogurt
- 2 Tbsp canola oil
- 1 large onion, diced
- 1 Tbsp garlic, minced
- 1 Tbsp ginger, grated
- 2 Tbsp tomato paste
- 1 can diced tomatoes
- ¾ cups chicken broth
- 1 cup heavy cream
- 1 tsp garlic powder
- 1 tsp onion powder
- 1 tsp ground turmeric
- 2 tsp garam masala
- 2 tsp red curry powder
- 1 tsp ground coriander
- 1 tsp ground cumin
- 2 tsp paprika
- 1 Tbsp kosher salt
- 2 cups white basmati rice, rinsed

INSTRUCTIONS:

1. Mix all the spices in a bowl.
2. Put the chicken into the bowl and add the yogurt and all of the spices.
3. Keep in the refrigerator for 24 hours.
4. Set to Sauté and heat the oil.
5. Add the chicken and sauté for 1 minute. Brown each side.
6. Add the onion. Sauté for 1 minute, stirring.
7. Add the garlic and ginger. Mix well.
8. Add the tomato paste and stir.
9. Add the diced tomatoes and the chicken broth. Stir gently to fully combine.

Orange Chicken Lettuce Wraps

Prep time: 5 minutes
Cooking time: 30 minutes
Servings: 4

NUTRIENTS PER SERVING:

Carbohydrates – 9 g
Fat – 5 g
Protein – 9 g
Calories – 112

INGREDIENTS:

- 2 pounds boneless and skinless chicken breasts, cubed
- 4 Tbsp cornstarch
- 2 Tbsp canola oil
- 1 Tbsp rice vinegar
- ⅓ cup water
- ¼ cup soy sauce
- 2 Tbsp brown sugar
- 1 Tbsp Asian sesame oil
- 1 tsp chili-garlic sauce
- 1 cup fresh orange juice
- 1 Tbsp grated orange zest
- Kosher salt and ground black pepper
- 2 small heads romaine lettuce leaves
- Sesame seeds

INSTRUCTIONS:

1. Toss the chicken with 2 Tbsp of the cornstarch in a bowl to coat evenly.
2. Set to Sauté and heat the oil.
3. Brown each side of chicken (5-6 minutes for 1 side).
4. Pour in the water and add the soy sauce, sugar, vinegar, sesame oil, chili-garlic sauce, and ½ cup of the orange juice. Stir well.
5. Lock the lid and set to 7 minutes of high pressure.
6. Do a natural release.
7. Mix ¼ cup of sauce, 3 Tbsp cornstarch, in a bowl add it to the pot.
8. Press Cancel and set to Sauté.
9. Let it simmer and cook to a thick sauce for 2-3 minutes.
10. Add in ½ cup orange juice, orange zest, salt, and pepper. Mix well.
11. Put the lettuce leaves on a serving platter.
12. Fill the leaves with chicken.
13. Sprinkle with toasted sesame seeds.
14. Enjoy!

MEAT

Hibachi Steak and Vegetables

Prep time: 5 minutes

Cooking time: 10 minutes

Servings: 2

NUTRIENTS PER SERVING:

Carbohydrates – 60 g

Fat – 2 g

Protein – 18 g

Calories – 297

INGREDIENTS:

- 1⅓ cup soy sauce
- 2 Tbsp white vinegar
- 1 Tbsp ginger, grated
- 1 clove garlic, minced
- 1 Tbsp granulated sugar
- ¼ tsp white pepper or black pepper
- 1 lbs 450 grams beef steak sirloin, cubed
- 1 zucchini sliced in rounds then halved
- 1 yellow onion diced
- 4 chestnut mushrooms sliced
- Parsley, chopped
- Sesame seeds toasted

INSTRUCTIONS:

1. Add the soy sauce, vinegar, ginger, garlic, sugar, and white pepper to the pot.
2. Add the steak, onion, zucchini, and mushrooms.
3. Lock the lid. Turn the valve to Sealing.
4. Set to 4 minutes of high pressure.
5. Do a quick-release.
6. If the sauce is not thick, take out the vegetables and stir in a slurry (1-2 tsp of cornstarch + 1-2 tsp of water). Cook for 2-3 minutes. Put the vegetables back in and mix well.
7. Serve with rice, sesame seeds, and parsley.
8. Enjoy!

Korean Beef

Prep time: 10 minutes

Cooking time: 15 minutes

Servings: 6

NUTRIENTS PER SERVING:

Carbohydrates – 42 g

Fat – 27 g

Protein – 21 g

Calories – 460

INGREDIENTS:

- ½ cup beef broth
- ⅓ cup soy sauce
- ⅓ cup brown sugar, packed
- 4 cloves garlic, minced
- 1 Tbsp sesame oil
- 1 Tbsp rice wine vinegar
- 1 Tbsp freshly grated ginger
- 1 tsp Sriracha
- ½ tsp onion powder
- ½ tsp white pepper
- 3 pounds boneless beef chuck roast, cubed
- 3 Tbsp cornstarch
- 1 tsp sesame seeds
- 2 green onions, thinly sliced

INSTRUCTIONS:

1. Mix the beef broth, rice wine vinegar, soy sauce, sesame oil, brown sugar, garlic, ginger, Sriracha, onion powder and white pepper in a bowl.
2. Put the chuck roast into the pot and add in the broth mixture. Stir well.
3. Lock the lid and set to 15 minutes of high pressure.
4. Do a quick-release.
5. Mix cornstarch and water in a bowl.
6. Set to Sauté (High). Add a slurry to make the sauce thicker and cook for 2-3 minutes.
7. Serve with green onions and sesame seeds.
8. Enjoy!

Korean Short Ribs

Prep time: 15 minutes

Cooking time: 55 minutes

Servings: 6

NUTRIENTS PER SERVING:

Carbohydrates – 21 g

Fat – 2 g

Protein – 2 g

Calories – 105

INGREDIENTS:

- 3.3 pounds bone-in beef short ribs
- 250g carrots, cut in chunks
- 200g Korean radish, cut in chunks
- For sauce:
- ½ cup water
- 1 red apple, cored chopped
- ½ onion, chopped
- 6 Tbsp soy sauce, regular
- 2 Tbsp brown sugar
- 2 Tbsp honey
- 2 Tbsp rice wine
- 1 Tbsp minced garlic
- 1 tsp sesame oil
- 5 whole black peppercorns

INSTRUCTIONS:

1. Boil the short ribs over medium-high heat for 6 to 8 minutes.

2. Rinse the ribs in cold water. Clean any excess fat from ribs and put them into the pot.
3. Mix the sauce ingredients in a mixer or food processor until smooth.
4. Pour the sauce over the ribs.
5. Lock the lid. Turn the valve to Sealing.
6. Set to 35 minutes of high pressure.
7. Do a natural release.
8. Take out the meat and cover with foil.
9. Add the vegetables to the pot and set to Sauté (Normal) and cook for 20 minutes.
10. Turn off and mix the vegetables with the meat. Toss to cover with sauce.
11. Serve with rice.
12. Enjoy!

Yukgaejang

Prep time: 5 minutes
Cooking time: 1 hour 10 minutes
Servings: 6

NUTRIENTS PER SERVING:

Carbohydrates – 11 g
Fat – 15 g
Protein – 21 g
Calories – 262

INGREDIENTS:

- 8 cups water
- 1 lb beef brisket, cut in half and soaked
- 2 green onions, cut into 2-inch lengths
- 12 oz mung bean sprouts, drained
- 2 eggs
- 1 onion medium size
- 3 garlic cloves
- 3 Tbsp sesame oil
- 2 Tbsp korean red chili pepper gochukaru
- 7 tsp guk ganjang
- 2 tsp sea salt
- 2 tsp chili oil (optional)
- 2 tsp gochujang
- 1 tsp sugar
- 2 Tbsp garlic, chopped
- 1.5 tsp garlic powder
- 1 tsp black pepper
- 2 tsp sesame seeds, crushed

INSTRUCTIONS:

1. Add the water, beef brisket, onion, and garlic cloves to the pot.
2. Lock the lid and set to 30 minutes of Meat.

3. Do a natural or quick-release.
4. Take out the meat and remove the onion and garlic cloves from the broth.
5. Shred the meat in a bowl and set aside.
6. Add the green onions and all the spices (except chili oil) to the meat. Mix well.
7. Put the meat back into the pot and cover with the green onion mixture.
8. Add the chili oil and scatter mung bean sprouts over the meat.
9. Lock the lid and set to 5 minutes of Soup.
10. Whip the eggs lightly, so that there are still streaks of egg white.
11. Do a quick-release and let it cool for 5 minutes.
12. Open the lid, set to Sauté, and boil for 30 minutes.
13. When the soup boils, add the eggs.
14. Serve and enjoy!

Massaman Beef Curry

Prep time: 15 minutes

Cooking time: 40 minutes

Servings: 4

NUTRIENTS PER SERVING:

Carbohydrates – 14 g

Fat – 8 g

Protein – 12 g

Calories – 183

INGREDIENTS:

- 1½ lb beef chunk, cut into 2-inch cubes
- 2½ cup coconut milk (not canned)
- 6 Tbsp massaman curry paste
- 3 Tbsp fish sauce
- 3 Tbsp palm sugar, chopped
- 3 Tbsp tamarind juice
- 1 potato, cut into chunks
- ½ onion, cut into strips
- ¼ cup roasted peanuts
- 3 tsp red curry paste
- 1 tsp coriander seeds toasted
- 1 tsp toasted cumin seeds, or ground
- ⅛ tsp ground nutmeg
- 1 tsp ground cinnamon
- ¼ tsp ground cloves
- ¼ tsp ground cardamom

INSTRUCTIONS:

1. Grind all whole spices into a powder with a mortar and pestle.
2. Mix the curry paste and ground spices together.
3. Set to Sauté and heat the oil.
4. Brown the meat on each side. Take it out.
5. Pour in ½ cup coconut milk and let it boil.
6. Add the paste and mix well. Cool until it gets thicker, stirring occasionally.
7. Pour in the rest of the coconut milk. Add the beef, deglazed pan juice, fish sauce, palm sugar, and tamarind. Mix well.
8. Lock the lid and set to 30 minutes of high pressure.
9. Do a natural and quick-release.
10. Add the potato, onions, and peanuts.
11. Set to Sauté and let it and simmer. Cook until potatoes are done.
12. Serve with rice.
13. Enjoy!

Vietnamese Beef Pho

Prep time: 10 minutes

Cooking time: 40 minutes

Servings: 7

NUTRIENTS PER SERVING:

Carbohydrates – 51 g

Fat – 6 g

Protein – 34 g

Calories – 367

INGREDIENTS:

- 1 large onion
- 5 to 6 cloves garlic
- 1 bunch of carrots, chopped
- 1 apple, peeled and chopped
- 1 cinnamon stick
- 1 Tbsp fennel seeds
- 4 to 5 cloves
- 1-inch ginger, sliced
- 1 tsp black peppercorns
- 1 tsp salt
- 1 tsp fish sauce
- 1 lb sirloin tips
- 3 cups beef bone broth
- 5 cups water
- Rice noodles, prepared
- 2 carrots, sliced
- 2 peppers, sliced
- A pinch of cilantro, cilantro
- Pieces of lime, sliced

INSTRUCTIONS:

1. Set to Sauté and heat the oil.
2. Add the onions, carrots, garlic, cinnamon stick, fennel, cloves, peppercorns, and salt. Cook for 2 to 3 minutes.
3. Add the sirloin tips and bone broth. Pour water into the pot.
4. Lock the lid and set to 25 minutes of high pressure.
5. Do a natural release.
6. Strain the pho broth over a large colander.
7. Take out the meat and add it to the bowls with the rice noodles.
8. Remove mushy onions and carrots and add the fish sauce.
9. Pour the pho broth over the rice noodles.
10. Serve with a piece of lime and chopped cilantro! Enjoy!

Vietnamese Bo Kho

Prep time: 10 minutes

Cooking time: 30 minutes

Servings: 6

NUTRIENTS PER SERVING:

Carbohydrates – 8 g

Fat – 9 g

Protein – 15 g

Calories – 175

INGREDIENTS:

- 1 onion
- 1 pound beef stew meat
- 2 Tbsp tomato paste
- 2 whole star anise
- 1 Tbsp lemongrass paste
- 1 Tbsp ginger, minced
- 1 Tbsp garlic, minced
- 1½ cup water
- 5 cups coconut water
- 1 tsp ground black pepper
- ½ tsp Chinese 5 spice powder
- ½ tsp curry powder
- 1 turnip, chopped into quarters
- 2 carrots, chopped into thick chunks
- ¼ cup water

INSTRUCTIONS:

1. Mix the carrots, turnip, and water in a heatproof bowl.
2. Add the rest of the ingredients to the pot.
3. Put a steamer rack over the meat.
4. Place the bowl of vegetables on the steamer rack.
5. Lock the lid and set to 15 minutes of high pressure.
6. Do a natural release.
7. Serve with fresh cilantro.
8. Enjoy!

Caramelized Pork

Prep time: 15 minutes

Cooking time: 40 minutes

Servings: 6

NUTRIENTS PER SERVING:

Carbohydrates – 20 g

Fat – 11 g

Protein – 35 g

Calories – 320

INGREDIENTS:

- 2 Tbsp canola oil
- 2 lb pork butt cut in 1-inch pieces
- Salt and ground black pepper as required
- 4 Tbsp brown sugar
- 3 garlic cloves minced
- 2 Tbsp fish sauce
- ½ cup water
- ½ cup chicken broth
- 1 small onion sliced
- 1 scallion chopped

INSTRUCTIONS:

1. Set to Sauté and heat the oil.
2. Add the pork, salt, and pepper. Brown each side of meat (5-6 minutes).
3. Add the sugar and sauté for 2 minutes, whilst stirring.
4. Add the garlic and cook for 1 minute.
5. Turn off and pour in the broth, water, and fish sauce.
6. Lock the lid. Turn the valve to Sealing.
7. Set to 20 minutes of high pressure.
8. Do a natural and quick-release.
9. Set to Sauté and add the onions. Cook for 5-10 minutes.
10. Serve with chopped scallions.

Banh Mi

Prep time: 5 minutes
Cooking time: 1 hour 25 minutes
Servings: 6

NUTRIENTS PER SERVING:

Carbohydrates – 46 g
Fat – 18 g
Protein – 14 g
Calories – 391

INGREDIENTS:

- 1 Tbsp lime juice
- ¼ cup fish sauce
- 1 Tbsp garlic minced
- 1 tsp black pepper ground
- 1 tsp Chinese five-spice powder
- 2 Tbsp sugar
- 2.5 lbs pork butt
- 1 Tbsp vegetable oil
- 6 little French baguettes, cut in half
- Butter
- Sriracha mayonnaise
- Pâté
- Pickled julienned daikon and carrots
- Thinly sliced English cucumber
- Maggi seasoning sauce
- Cilantro leaves
- Sliced jalapeno

INSTRUCTIONS:

1. Mix the lime juice, fish sauce, garlic, black pepper, Chinese 5-spice powder, and sugar in a bowl.
2. Put the pork into the pot and coat it with the sauce.
3. Set to 60 minutes of pressure cook.
4. Do a natural release.
5. Take out the meat and shred with forks. Remove the fat. Reserve the liquid.
6. Shred the meat using two forks, and remove any visible fat.
7. Set to Sauté and heat the oil.
8. Add 2 cups of meat and brown each side.
9. Add 2 tsp cooking liquid. Turn off.
10. Spread butter on both halves of the baguettes.
11. Toast both sides of bread in the oven on a tray.
12. Spread the mayonnaise on one half of bread.
13. Spread the pâté on the other half.
14. In layers, put the pork, pickled daikon, carrots, a few drops of Maggi sauce, cilantro, sliced jalapenos on the bottom half.
15. Top with the other half of bread.
16. Serve and enjoy!

Beef Rendang

Prep time: 10 minutes
Cooking time: 30 minutes
Servings: 6

NUTRIENTS PER SERVING:

Carbohydrates – 15 g
Fat – 19 g
Protein – 55 g
Calories – 447

INGREDIENTS:

- 1½ cup water
- 1 stick of cinnamon
- 3 whole cloves
- 3 whole star anise
- 3 green cardamom pods
- 4 stalks lemongrass, chopped
- 6 shallots, peeled and chopped
- 1 piece galangal, peeled and chopped
- 1 piece ginger, peeled and chopped
- 6 cloves garlic
- 20 dried Japanese chilis
- 2 tsp ground cumin
- 2 tsp ground coriander
- 2 tsp fennel seeds
- 3 candlenuts or 6 macadamia nuts
- 1 2" piece turmeric, peeled
- 3 lbs beef chuck, cut
- 4–5 Tbsp coconut oil
- 1 can coconut milk
- ¼ cup tamarind concentrate
- 6 kaffir lime leaves, sliced
- 1–2 Tbsp sugar

INSTRUCTIONS:

1. Add all the spice paste ingredients to the blender and blend until smooth.
2. Set to Sauté and heat the coconut oil.
3. Add and Sauté the spice paste for 2 minutes.
4. Add water to deglaze the pot.
5. Add the remaining sauce ingredients (except salt). Stir to combine well.
6. Lock the lid. Turn the valve to Sealing.
7. Set to 20 minutes of high pressure.
8. Do a natural release.
9. Set to Sauté and reduce until almost no sauce is left and it is a deep brown.
10. Serve hot and enjoy!

Szechuan Beef

Prep time: 10 minutes

Cooking time: 25 minutes

Servings: 4

NUTRIENTS PER SERVING:

Carbohydrates – 18 g

Fat – 4 g

Protein – 28 g

Calories – 210

INGREDIENTS:

- 2 lbs beef stir fry meat
- 1 cup beef broth
- 1 Tbsp garlic, minced
- 3 Tbsp garlic chili sauce
- 1 tsp ginger, grated
- 3 Tbsp soy sauce
- 1 Tbsp cornstarch
- 1½ cups spring onions, diced
- 2 red bell peppers, diced
- 1 cup carrots, shredded
- 6 mushrooms, sliced

INSTRUCTIONS:

1. Set to Sauté and add the beef to the pot.
2. Add the beef broth and sear the meat.
3. Press Cancel, Lock the lid. Turn the valve to Sealing.
4. Set to 20 minutes of high pressure.
5. Do a quick-release.
6. Drain juice from the pot.
7. Replace back into the instant pot.
8. Mix the chili sauce, ginger, garlic, soy sauce. Gradually add the cornstarch.
9. Set to Sauté, pour in the sauce, and cover the meat.
10. Add the vegetables and cook for 3 minutes.
11. Turn off the Instant Pot.
12. Serve with rice.
13. Enjoy!

Char Siu – Chinese BBQ Pork

Prep time: 10 minutes
Cooking time: 45 minutes
Servings: 2-4

NUTRIENTS PER SERVING:

Carbohydrates – 10 g
Fat – 11 g
Protein – 15 g
Calories – 192

INGREDIENTS:

- 1 pound pork butt meat, split the longer side in half
- 3 Tbsp honey
- 2 Tbsp light soy sauce
- 1 cup water
- A pinch Kosher salt to season
- For marinade:
- 1 Tbsp chu hou paste
- 2 cubes Chinese fermented red bean curd
- 3 Tbsp char siu sauce
- ½ tsp sesame oil
- 2 Tbsp Shaoxing wine
- 1 tsp garlic powder
- 1 Tbsp light soy sauce

INSTRUCTIONS:

1. Pierce holes all over the pork with a fork.
2. Mix all of the marinade ingredients and pour in the mixture to a ziplock.
3. Add the meat to the ziplock and squeeze the air out. Marinate for 30 minutes.
4. Take out the pork and marinade from the bag.
5. Add 1 cup of water into the bag and mix it with the remaining marinade.
6. Pour the marinade mixture into the pot.
7. Put the meat into a steamer rack it.
8. Season the pork with salt on both sides.
9. Lock the lid and set to 18 minutes of high pressure.
10. Do a natural release.
11. Combine the light soy sauce and honey in a bowl. Coat meat with sauce.
12. Put the pork into a preheated oven (450°F) and cook for 4 - 6 minutes to brown the honey.
13. Serve with rice and honey sauce.

Indian Curry Lamb

Prep time: 10 minutes

Cooking time: 35 minutes

Servings: 4

NUTRIENTS PER SERVING:

Carbohydrates – 4 g

Fat – 14 g

Protein – 28 g

Calories – 259

INGREDIENTS:

- 2½ pounds lamb spare ribs
- 2 tsp kosher salt
- 1 Tbsp Indian curry powder
- For sauce:
- 1 Tbsp ghee
- 1 yellow onion, chopped
- ½ pound tomatoes, chopped
- 5 garlic cloves, minced
- 1 Tbsp Indian curry powder
- 1 Tbsp kosher salt
- 2 Tbsp lemon juice
- 1¼ cup chopped cilantro, divided
- ¼ cup of cilantro, chopped

INSTRUCTIONS:

1. Season the lamb spare ribs with salt and curry powder. Cover and put into the fridge for 4-24 hours.
2. Set to Sauté and melt the ghee.
3. Brown the ribs in two batches. Transfer to a plate when the ribs are done.
4. Put the onion and tomatoes into a blender to make a smooth puree.
5. Add the garlic to the empty pot. Sauté for 20 seconds and then add the tomato and onion puree.
6. Add the rest of the sauce ingredients and put the seared lamb spare ribs back in the pot.
7. Lock the lid and set to 20 minutes of high pressure.
8. Do a natural release.
9. Serve with chopped cilantro.
10. Enjoy!

Bacon Ramen

Prep time: 5 minutes
Cooking time: 25 minutes
Servings: 5

NUTRIENTS PER SERVING:

Carbohydrates – 40 g

Fat – 25 g

Protein – 21 g

Calories – 487

INGREDIENTS:

- ½ package of bacon, chopped
- 1 inch ginger, minced
- 8 ounces mushrooms, sliced
- 5 cups chicken broth
- 2 Tbsp soy sauce
- ¼ cup rice vinegar
- 1 Tbsp red curry paste
- 1 Tbsp toasted sesame oil
- 2 frozen boneless, skinless chicken breasts
- 5 oz. noodles
- 1 cups fresh baby spinach
- A pinch of green onion, chopped
- A pinch of sesame seeds, toasted

INSTRUCTIONS:

1. Set to Sauté and add bacon. Sauté bacon until crispy.
2. Transfer cooked bacon to a paper towel- lined plate. Set aside.
3. Add the ginger and mushrooms to the pot, and Sauté for 1-2 minutes, stirring occasionally. Press Cancel.
4. Pour in the broth, soy sauce, rice vinegar, red curry paste, sesame oil and add the chicken breasts.
5. Lock the lid. Turn the valve to Sealing.
6. Set to 15 minutes of high pressure.
7. Do a quick-release.
8. Add the noodles and spinach.
9. Allow the noodles to soften in the hot soup.
10. Take out the chicken and shred it. Put the shredded chicken back into the pot.
11. Serve the ramen with sesame seeds and chopped green onion. Enjoy!

FISH & SEAFOOD

Vietnamese Salmon

Prep time: 5 hours

Cooking time: 15 minutes

Servings: 4

NUTRIENTS PER SERVING:

Carbohydrates – 18 g

Fat – 14 g

Protein – 35 g

Calories – 259

INGREDIENTS:

- 1 Tbsp olive oil
- ⅓ cup light brown sugar packed
- 3 Tbsp Asian fish sauce
- 1½ Tbsp soy sauce
- ½ tsp ginger grated
- 1 lime grated zest
- ½ lime juice
- ½ tsp black pepper
- 4 fresh skinless salmon fillets
- Green onion, sliced
- Fresh cilantro leaves

INSTRUCTIONS:

1. Set to Sauté and add the oil, brown sugar, soy sauce, fish sauce, lime zest, ginger, lime juice, and pepper to the pot. Let it simmer and press Cancel.
2. Put the fish into the pot with the skin side up. Add some sauce over the fish.
3. Lock the lid and set to 1 minute of low pressure.
4. Do a natural release.
5. Set to Saute (Normal) and cook fish for 1 minute.
6. Transfer the salmon to the plate with the other side up.
7. Cook the sauce for another 3 minutes.
8. Cover the salmon with sauce.
9. Serve with green onion, cilantro leaves and lime pieces.

Shrimp Tempura

Prep time: 5 minutes

Cooking time: 15 minutes

Servings: 4

NUTRIENTS PER SERVING:

Carbohydrates – 11 g

Fat – 9 g

Protein – 6 g

Calories – 152

INGREDIENTS:

- 1 pound of shrimp
- 1 cup panko breadcrumbs
- 1 cup all-purpose flour
- ½ tsp powdered garlic
- 1½ tsp black pepper
- 1 tsp smoked paprika
- ½ tsp salt
- 2 eggs, beaten
- ¼ vegetable oil, for frying

INSTRUCTIONS:

1. Mix the garlic powder, salt, and black pepper in a bowl.
2. Add the shrimp and coat them with the spice mix.
3. In another bowl, mix the all-purpose flour and smoked paprika well.
4. Beat the eggs in a new bowl.
5. Add the panko breadcrumbs to another bowl.
6. Set to Sauté and heat the oil.
7. Dip the shrimp into the flour mix, then into the beaten eggs.
8. Toss in panko to coat all sides.
9. Put the shrimp into the hot oil.
10. Sauté for 5 minutes (until golden).
11. Take out and put on the plate to drain.
12. Serve and enjoy!

Chao Ca – Vietnamese Fish Congee

Prep time: 5 minutes

Cooking time: 25 minutes

Servings: 4

NUTRIENTS PER SERVING:

Carbohydrates – 56 g

Fat – 6 g

Protein – 8 g

Calories – 310

INGREDIENTS:

- ¾ cup rice
- 2 Tbsp split mung, washed and drained
- 1 - 1.5 lb fish bones, scrubbed with salt and rinsed
- A thumb-sized piece of ginger, sliced
- 1 large shallot, cut in half
- 6 cups water
- 1 tsp salt
- 1 Tbsp fish sauce
- 1 lb fish fillet, sliced into ½ in thick pieces
- A pinch of green onion, chopped
- Fresh cilantro

INSTRUCTIONS:

1. Add the mung beans, rice, fish bones, ginger, shallot, water, and salt to the pot.
2. Lock the lid and set to 12 minutes of high pressure.
3. Season the fillet slices with salt and pepper. Set aside.
4. Do a natural release.
5. Remove the fish bones.
6. Set to Sauté and add the fillet slices. Cook until the fish is fully cooked.
7. Add fish sauce and seasoning to your taste if needed.
8. Serve with chopped green onion and cilantro. Enjoy!

Coconut Caramel Shrimp

Prep time: 10 minutes

Cooking time: 25 minutes

Servings: 4

NUTRIENTS PER SERVING:

Carbohydrates – 26 g

Fat – 2 g

Protein – 20 g

Calories – 194

INGREDIENTS:

- 3 Tbsp coconut water
- 7 Tbsp white sugar
- ¼ cup fish sauce
- 1 pound medium shrimp, peeled and deveined
- 2 Tbsp ginger, minced
- 1 Tbsp garlic, grated
- ¼ tsp black pepper
- 2 tsp tapioca flour

INSTRUCTIONS:

1. Set to Sauté and add 3 Tbsp of coconut water and sugar. Stir and let it bubble.
2. Microwave ½ cup coconut water to heat it for 1-3 minutes.
3. Gradually pour the hot coconut water into the pot.
4. Add in the fish sauce and shrimp. Hit Cancel.
5. Lock the lid. Turn the valve to Sealing.
6. Set to 3 minutes of high pressure.
7. Do a quick-release.
8. Add the ginger, garlic, and pepper. Mix well.
9. Press Cancel and set to Sauté.
10. Add the tapioca flour and whisk thoroughly.
11. Cook for 2 minutes, to make sauce thicker.
12. Serve hot. Enjoy!

Vietnamese Caramel Salmon

Prep time: 5 minutes

Cooking time: 5 minutes

Servings: 4

NUTRIENTS PER SERVING:

Carbohydrates – 22 g

Fat – 14 g

Protein – 34 g

Calories – 337

INGREDIENTS:

- 1 Tbsp olive oil or coconut oil
- ⅓ cup packed light brown sugar
- 3 Tbsp Asian fish sauce
- 2 Tbsp lime juice
- 1½ Tbsp soy sauce
- 1 tsp ginger grated
- 1 tsp lime zest
- ½ tsp black pepper
- 4 6 oz. salmon fillets
- 1 pinch chopped cilantro
- 1 pinch sliced onion

INSTRUCTIONS:

1. Set to Sauté and heat the oil.
2. Add the sugar, fish sauce, lime juice, soy sauce, ginger, lime zest, and black pepper. Mix well.
3. Let it simmer and press Cancel.
4. Add the salmon, skin-side up. Spoon the sauce over the salmon.
5. Set to 1 minute of low pressure. pressure for 1 minute.
6. Do a natural and quick-release.
7. Transfer the salmon to the plate with the skin side down.
8. Set to Sauté and cook the sauce for 2-3 minutes to make it thicker.
9. Serve with the sauce over the fish, chopped cilantro and sliced green onions.

Coconut Mahi-Mahi

Prep time: 5 minutes

Cooking time: 25 minutes

Servings: 4

NUTRIENTS PER SERVING:

Carbohydrates – 9 g

Fat – 7 g

Protein – 22 g

Calories – 186

INGREDIENTS:

- 1 Tbsp plain sesame oil
- 2 shallots, washed and minced
- 2 Tbsp grated fresh ginger
- ½ cup coarsely chopped fresh cilantro
- 1 stalk lemongrass, chopped
- 1 Tbsp Asian fish sauce
- 14 oz can unsweetened coconut milk
- 4 mahi-mahi fillets
- black pepper to taste
- 4 green onions, sliced
- 2 limes, quartered

INSTRUCTIONS:

1. Set to Sauté (Normal) and heat the oil.
2. Add shallots. Cook for 2 minutes, stirring occasionally.
3. Set to Sauté (Low).
4. Add the ginger, cilantro, lemongrass, fish sauce, coconut milk. Let it simmer.
5. Using a spatula, lower the mahi-mahi fillets into the hot liquid.
6. Lock the lid. Turn the valve to Sealing.
7. Set to 3 minutes of high pressure.
8. Do a natural release.
9. Take out and transfer fillets to a serving platter.
10. Remove the lemongrass and cilantro stems.
11. Coat fish fillets with coconut sauce.
12. Season to taste with black pepper.
13. Serve over cooked rice. Enjoy!

Indian Butter Shrimp

Prep time: 10 minutes
Cooking time: 45 minutes
Servings: 6

NUTRIENTS PER SERVING:

Carbohydrates – 8 g
Fat – 24 g
Protein – 8 g
Calories – 259

INGREDIENTS:

- 1¼ cup plain whole-milk yogurt
- 2 tsp ground cumin
- 2 tsp sweet smoked paprika
- 2 tsp garam masala
- 2 tsp fresh lime juice
- 1½ tsp kosher salt
- 1 tsp grated ginger
- 1 garlic clove, minced
- 2 pounds shrimp, peeled and deveined
- 4 Tbsp butter
- 2 shallots, minced
- 2 garlic cloves, minced
- 1½ tsp ginger, grated
- ¼ to ½ tsp crushed red pepper flakes
- ¼ tsp salt
- 1 28-ounce can diced tomatoes
- 1 cup heavy cream
- ½ tsp lime zest

INSTRUCTIONS:

1. Combine the yogurt, cumin, paprika, garam masala, lime juice, salt, ginger, and garlic.

2. Add the shrimp, cover the bowl and put it into the fridge for 1 hour.
3. Set to Sauté and melt the butter.
4. Add shallots and salt. Sauté for 4-8 minutes.
5. Add in the garlic, ginger, red pepper flakes, and ¼ tsp salt. Cook for 1 to 2 minutes.
6. Add the tomatoes, cream and salt.
7. Set to Sauté (High) and let it boil.
8. Set to 8 minutes of high pressure.
9. Do a quick-release.
10. Set to Sauté and let the sauce simmer. Cook for 5-7 minutes until it gets thicker.
11. Add the shrimp, liquid from the bowl, 2 Tbsp butter, and lime zest.
12. Cook until the shrimp are pink (2-5 minutes).
13. Serve with rice and fresh cilantro.
14. Enjoy!

Asaam Pedas Fish

Prep time: 5 minutes

Cooking time: 15 minutes

Servings: 4

NUTRIENTS PER SERVING:

Carbohydrates – 12 g

Fat – 17 g

Protein – 3 g

Calories – 213

INGREDIENTS:

- 10 okras
- 1 tsp fish curry powder
- 2 sprigs Vietnamese coriander
- 1 pomfret, ½ pound to 1 pound
- 5 Tbsp cooking oil
- 1 tomato, cut into wedges
- 1 Tbsp sugar
- Salt to taste

Spice Paste:

- 1 clove garlic
- 1 stalk of lemongrass, white part only
- 4 shallots
- 8 dried chilies
- ½ Tbsp belacan, prawn paste
- 1¼ cup water
- Tamarind pulp, soaked and squeezed to get juice

INSTRUCTIONS:

1. Add all of the spice ingredients into a food processor to grind them. Set aside.
2. Set to Sauté and heat the oil.
3. Add the paste and cook for 2 minutes.
4. Add the tamarind juice and fish curry powder.
5. Add the tomato wedges, okra and daun kesom.
6. When it starts to boil, add the fish, salt, and sugar.
7. Simmer until the fish is cooked.
8. Serve hot.
9. Enjoy!

Steamed Sea Bass

Prep time: 15 minutes

Cooking time: 5 minutes

Servings: 4

NUTRIENTS PER SERVING:

Carbohydrates – 0 g

Fat – 2 g

Protein – 23 g

Calories – 125

INGREDIENTS:

- 1 tsp garlic minced
- 1 tsp fresh ginger minced
- 2 Tbsp rice wine
- 1 Tbsp soy sauce
- 1 Tbsp fish sauce
- Freshly ground black pepper as required
- 1 lb whole sea bass
- 2 cups water
- 1 tsp fresh ginger julienned finely
- ¼ cup light soy sauce
- 1 Tbsp water
- 1 scallion julienned
- ¼ cup canola oil

INSTRUCTIONS:

1. Combine all of the ingredients (except the fish and water) in a baking dish and mix well.
2. Add the fish and set aside for 20-30 minutes.
3. Put the steamer basket into the pot and pour in water.
4. Put the fish in the steamer basket.
5. Lock the lid. Turn the valve to Sealing.
6. Set to 2 minutes of low pressure.
7. Do a quick release.
8. Mix the ginger, soy sauce, wine, and 1 Tbsp of water in a bowl.
9. Transfer the fish to the serving plate.
10. Cover the fish with ginger sauce.
11. Now, arrange the scallions over the fish.
12. Heat the pan with oil and pour it over the fish.
13. Serve and enjoy!

Steamed Fish with Ginger

Prep time: 10 minutes
Cooking time: 30 minutes
Servings: 2

NUTRIENTS PER SERVING:

Carbohydrates – 20 g
Fat – 10 g
Protein – 10 g
Calories – 210

INGREDIENTS:

- 1 whole red snapper cleaned, gutted, scales removed, tail trimmed
- 1 Tbsp calamansi
- 1 Tbsp Xiao Xing rice wine
- 1 Tbsp soy sauce
- 1 tsp salt
- 1 tsp ground black pepper powder
- 1 whole white or yellow onion, chopped
- 2 stalks scallions, chopped
- 1 inch ginger, peeled and sliced
- ½ tsp sesame oil
- 1 Tbsp chopped fresh parsley for garnish
- 2 Tbsp patis (fish sauce) served as side dipping sauce
- ½ tsp black peppercorns
- 1 whole fresh lemon sliced, for garnish

INSTRUCTIONS:

1. Wash and dry the fish with paper towels.
2. Make 2-3 slits in the middle part of whole fish.
3. Put lemon juice, rice wine, soy sauce, salt, black pepper inside the fish and marinate for ONLY 30 minutes.
4. Mix the onions, scallions, ginger and black peppercorns in a bowl. Put inside the fish.
5. Add the sesame oil on top of and inside the fish.
6. Put fish and ingredients in a prepared round pan.
7. pour 3 cups of water into the pot.
8. Lock the lid. Turn the valve to Sealing.
9. Set to 10 minutes of high pressure.
10. Do a quick-release.
11. Transfer the fish to a serving plate and add the greens.
12. Serve with rice. Enjoy!

Panko-Crusted Cod

Prep time: 10 minutes

Cooking time: 10 minutes

Servings: 4

NUTRIENTS PER SERVING:

Carbohydrates – 10 g

Fat – 11 g

Protein – 31 g

Calories – 270

INGREDIENTS:

- ½ cup panko bread crumbs
- 2 Tbsp extra-virgin olive oil
- 2 tsp grated lemon zest
- ¼ tsp salt
- ¼ cup light mayonnaise
- 2 tsp lemon juice
- ½ tsp dried thyme
- 4 6 oz cod fillets
- 1 cup Water
- 1 lemon cut into 4 wedges

INSTRUCTIONS:

1. Set to Sauté (High) and heat the pot.
2. Add the bread crumbs and sauté for 2 minutes, stirring frequently.
3. Add the oil, lemon zest, and salt. Transfer to a plate and set aside.
4. Mix the mayonnaise, lemon juice, and thyme in a bowl.
5. Spread the mixture over the top of the cod fillets.
6. Pour water into the pot and put the fish into the steamer basket, mayonnaise side up.
7. Lock the lid and set to 3 minutes of Manual.
8. Do a quick-release.
9. Serve the fish topped with the bread crumb mixture and lemon wedges.
10. Enjoy!

Sambal Udang – Prawn Sandal

Prep time: 20 minutes
Cooking time: 20 minutes
Servings: 6

NUTRIENTS PER SERVING:

Carbohydrates – 13 g
Fat – 15 g
Protein – 49 g
Calories – 248

INGREDIENTS:

- 4 Tbsp vegetable oil
- 1 lb prawns, peeled and deveined
- 6 kaffir lime leaves
- 2 Tbsp sugar
- 1½ tsp salt
- 3 cloves garlic, peeled
- 1 cup hot water
- 30 g tamarind paste, rinsed
- For the spice paste:
- 6 red chilies, seeded and cut into small pieces
- 8 dried chilies
- 2 stalks lemongrass, sliced
- 1 inch lengkuas, sliced
- 6 macadamias
- 1 medium onion, peeled and diced
- ½ cup water
- ¾ inch cube belacan, toasted

INSTRUCTIONS:

1. Add all of the spice paste ingredients to a blender to make a smooth paste.
2. Put the asam jawa in a strainer over a bowl.
3. Pour hot water over the asam jawa.
4. Mix and press down with a spoon to dissolve.
5. Set to Sauté and heat the oil.
6. Add the spice paste and kaffir lime leaves. Cook for 8-10 minutes.
7. Pour the strained tamarind juice into the pot. Stir to combine.
8. Cover the lid to let it boil.
9. Simmer for 3 to 5 minutes.
10. Open the lid and add the prawns, sugar and salt.
11. Mix well to combine.
12. Put the lid back on and cook for 3 minutes.
13. Serve hot and enjoy!

Shrimp with Lobster Sauce

Prep time: 10 minutes
Cooking time: 10 minutes
Servings: 4

NUTRIENTS PER SERVING:

Carbohydrates – 10 g
Fat – 11 g
Protein – 31 g
Calories – 270

INGREDIENTS:

- ½-1½ lbs raw large shrimp, peeled/shelled, tails off and deveined
- 1.5 cups lobster broth
- ½ Tbsp low sodium soy sauce
- ½ Tbsp Shaoxing wine
- 1 tsp of sugar
- ½ tsp white pepper
- ½ Tbsp crushed ginger
- ½ Tbsp crushed garlic
- 1.5 cups frozen peas
- 1 bunch of scallions, sliced
- 3 tablespoon cornstarch
- 3 tablespoons water
- 2 egg whites without yolks, beaten
- ½ Tbsp of heavy cream

INSTRUCTIONS:

1. Add the lobster broth, Shaoxing wine, soy sauce, ginger, garlic, sugar and white pepper to the pot. Mix well
2. Add the shrimp. Mix well.
3. Lock the lid. Turn the valve to Sealing.
4. Set to 0 minutes of high pressure.
5. Do a quick-release.
6. Meanwhile, beat the egg whites.
7. Make a cornstarch slurry to thicken the sauce.
8. Transfer the shrimp to a serving plate.
9. Set to Sauté (High) and let it boil.
10. Add the frozen peas and scallions and mix well.
11. When it starts bubbling, add the cornstarch slurry and mix for 1 minute.
12. Turn off and let it cool down.
13. When it has stopped bubbling, add beaten egg whites and stir.
14. Add the heavy cream and give it a stir.
15. Serve the shrimp with the sauce.

RICE & NOODLES

Japanese Fried Rice

Prep time: 10 minutes

Cooking time: 20 minutes

Servings: 4

NUTRIENTS PER SERVING:

Carbohydrates – 25 g

Fat – 12 g

Protein – 7 g

Calories – 240

INGREDIENTS:

- 2 cups grain rice, rinsed and drained
- 1 small onion, finely diced
- 10 oz frozen vegetable mix thawed
- 1¾ cups water
- 2 Tbsp low sodium soy sauce
- 1 Tbsp sesame oil
- 3-4 strips bacon, cut into ½ inch pieces
- 1 Tbsp chicken broth
- 1 tsp garlic paste
- 1 tsp ginger paste
- 2 eggs lightly beaten
- Salt and white pepper to taste
- 3-4 green onions finely chopped

INSTRUCTIONS:

1. Set to Sauté and add the bacon. Cook until it gets brown.
2. Add the onion. Cook for 2 minutes, stirring occasionally.
3. Add the garlic and ginger and stir for about 20 seconds. Turn off.
4. Add the rice and mix to coat it.
5. Add the water, soy sauce, vegetables, sesame oil, chicken broth and mix well.
6. Lock the lid. Turn the valve to Sealing.
7. Set to 5 minutes of high pressure.
8. Do a natural release.
9. Push the rice to one side of the pot and add the beaten eggs.
10. Scramble eggs for 2 minutes and fold into the rice until the eggs are cooked.
11. Serve with chopped green onions

Hibachi Fried Rice

Prep time: 5 hours

Cooking time: 30 minutes

Servings: 4

NUTRIENTS PER SERVING:

Carbohydrates – 45 g

Fat – 5 g

Protein – 7 g

Calories – 250

INGREDIENTS:

- 2 cups jasmine rice, rinsed well and drained
- 2 cups water
- 2 Tbsp sesame oil
- 2 Tbsp soy sauce
- 1 Tbsp butter
- 3 eggs
- ½ white onion, chopped
- 1 cup frozen peas and carrots, mixed
- 1 pinch of sesame seeds, toasted

INSTRUCTIONS:

1. Add the rice and water to the pot and stir well.
2. Lock the lid and set to 3 minutes of high pressure.
3. Do a natural release.
4. Transfer the rice to a bowl and fluff. Set aside.
5. Set to Sauté (Normal) and heat the sesame oil.
6. Add the onion. Cook for 1 minute.
7. Add the peas, carrots and corn.
8. Add the butter. Cook for 2 minutes.
9. Push the vegetables to one side of the pot and beat the eggs. Stir them to scramble and cook. When eggs start to cook, mix with veggies done.
10. Press Cancel, add the rice back in and add the soy sauce and sesame seeds.
11. Mix well with the veggies and eggs.
12. Serve with sesame seeds. Enjoy!

Chicken Pad Thai

Prep time: 15 minutes

Cooking time: 15 minutes

Servings: 4

NUTRIENTS PER SERVING:

Carbohydrates – 48 g

Fat – 16 g

Protein – 25 g

Calories – 402

INGREDIENTS:

- ½ Tbsp olive oil
- 2 chicken breasts, diced
- 4 cloves garlic, minced
- 3 Tbsp low-sodium soy sauce
- ½ cup jarred pad thai sauce
- 1½ cups water
- 7 oz rice noodles
- 1 cup carrot matchsticks
- ½ red + yellow pepper, sliced
- 4 green onions, sliced
- ⅓ cup peanuts, chopped
- ⅓ cup fresh cilantro, chopped

INSTRUCTIONS:

1. Add the olive oil, chicken, garlic, soy sauce, pad thai sauce, water and rice noodles to the pot (in that order).
2. Place noodles slightly above the other ingredients.
3. Set to 2 minutes of high pressure.
4. Do a quick-release.
5. Add the carrot matchsticks, bell peppers, and ½ of the peanuts, stirring carefully.
6. Cover with the lid for 5 minutes and then remove it.
7. Serve with green onions, chopped peanuts and cilantro. Enjoy!

Chicken Rice Bowls

Prep time: 30 minutes

Cooking time: 10 minutes

Servings: 4

NUTRIENTS PER SERVING:

Carbohydrates – 31 g

Fat – 15 g

Protein – 52 g

Calories – 477

INGREDIENTS:

- 2 Tbsp olive oil
- 4 chicken breasts
- 1 cup long-grain white rice
- 2 cups broth
- ½ cup sweet chili Thai sauce
- 3 Tbsp soy sauce
- ½ Tbsp fish sauce
- ½ Tbsp ginger, minced
- ½ Tbsp garlic, minced
- 1 tsp lime juice
- 1 tsp sriracha
- Cilantro optional garnish
- Shredded zucchini (optional)
- Peanuts (optional)

INSTRUCTIONS:

1. Set to Sauté and heat the olive oil.
2. Cook the chicken breasts for 2-3 minutes on each side.
3. Transfer the chicken to a glass baking dish.
4. Combine the Thai sweet chili sauce, soy sauce, fish sauce, ginger, garlic, lime juice and sriracha in a bowl.
5. Pour the sauce onto the chicken breasts.
6. Stir to combine.
7. Put the rice in the pot. Put the chicken and sauce on top.
8. Add the broth and lock the lid.
9. Set to 10 minutes of high pressure.
10. Do a natural release.
11. Shred the chicken with forks and stir the meat and rice together.
12. Serve with cilantro, sliced zucchini and peanuts. Enjoy!

Bang Bang Shrimp Pasta

Prep time: 5 minutes

Cooking time: 10 minutes

Servings: 6

NUTRIENTS PER SERVING:

Carbohydrates – 64 g

Fat – 17 g

Protein – 26 g

Calories – 495

INGREDIENTS:

- 1 pound dried spaghetti
- 3 cloves garlic, minced
- 1 tsp olive oil
- 1 tsp salt
- 4¼ cup water
- 1 pound cooked jumbo shrimp
- ½ cup mayonnaise
- ⅓ cup Thai sweet chili sauce
- 1 tsp smoked paprika
- ½ lime juice
- Salt and pepper
- 1 plus Tbsp sriracha sauce
- Dried green onions

INSTRUCTIONS:

1. Break the noodles in half and put into the pot.
2. Add the garlic, olive oil, salt and water.
3. Lock the lid and set to 4 minutes of high pressure.
4. Do a quick release.
5. Combine the mayonnaise, Thai sweet chili sauce, lime juice, and sriracha in a bowl.
6. Stir in the sauce and mix well to coat the noodles.
7. Add the shrimp to the sauce and mix well.
8. Set to Sauté and cook for 3-4 minutes.
9. Serve with dried green onions.

Chao Ga – Vietnamese Chicken Congee

Prep time: 5 minutes

Cooking time: 25 minutes

Servings: 4

NUTRIENTS PER SERVING:

Carbohydrates – 55 g

Fat – 23 g

Protein – 9 g

Calories – 284

INGREDIENTS:

- 1 cup jasmine rice, rinsed
- 6 cups of chicken broth
- 2 frozen skinless chicken breasts
- 4 garlic cloves, minced
- 1 knob of ginger, peeled
- 1 small or medium onion, peeled
- A pinch of green onion, chopped
- Ground black pepper, to taste

INSTRUCTIONS:

1. Add the rice, chicken broth, and frozen chicken breasts to the pot.
2. Add the garlic, onion and ginger to the pot.
3. Lock the lid and set to 25 minutes of high pressure.
4. Do a natural release.
5. Remove the onion and garlic from the porridge.
6. Take out the chicken breasts. Shred it and add back to the rice.
7. Serve with cilantro.
8. Enjoy!

Hainanese Chicken Rice

Prep time: 15 minutes

Cooking time: 10 minutes

Servings: 4

NUTRIENTS PER SERVING:

Carbohydrates – 38 g

Fat – 21 g

Protein – 11 g

Calories – 318

INGREDIENTS:

- 2 lbs boneless skin-on chicken thighs
- Salt to rub the chicken
- 2½ cups Jasmine Rice about, rinse and drain off water
- 1 cup chicken broth
- 1 Tbsp butter
- 2 pandan leaves tie into a knot
- A pinch of green onion, chopped
- 1 Tbsp soy sauce
- 1 tsp sesame oil

For paste:

- 6 cloves garlic, peeled
- 3 large shallots, peeled
- 1 ginger, peeled
- 1½ tsp salt
- 1 tsp sugar
- 3 Tbsp cooking oil

INSTRUCTIONS:

1. Put the garlic, shallots, ginger, salt, sugar, and oil in a food processor to make a paste.
2. Season the chicken with salt and then dry with a paper towel.
3. Set to Sauté and heat the aromatic paste. Sauté for 2-3 minutes.
4. Add in the broth. Press Cancel.
5. Add the butter then bouillon. Mix well.
6. Layer the chicken pieces, skin side up. Make sure the rice is covered with liquid.
7. Lock the lid. Turn the valve to Sealing.
8. Set to 8 minutes of high pressure.
9. Do a natural release.
10. Take out and transfer the meat to a plate.
11. Set to 5-7 minutes of high pressure again to reabsorb the liquid.
12. Mix 1 Tbsp soy sauce and 1 tsp sesame oil to brush the chicken for serving.
13. Serve with chopped green onion.

Nasi Lemak – Malay Coconut Milk Rice

Prep time: 5 minutes

Cooking time: 25 minutes

Servings: 4

NUTRIENTS PER SERVING:

Carbohydrates – 58 g

Fat – 13 g

Protein – 9 g

Calories – 400

INGREDIENTS:

- 1 tsp ginger puree
- 4 tsp garlic puree, divided
- ½ tsp puree turmeric
- 2 Tbsp dark soy sauce
- 1 Tbsp light soy sauce
- 1 Tbsp oyster flavored sauce
- A dash of sesame oil
- 1 tsp sugar
- Chicken thighs
- 1 cup water
- 2 cups basmati rice, rinsed and drained
- 3 cups coconut milk
- ½ tsp salt

INSTRUCTIONS:

1. Mix ginger, 2 tsp garlic puree, turmeric, soy and oyster sauces, and sesame oil in a bowl.
2. Marinate the meat in the mixture for 1-24 hours.
3. Place a trivet into the pot and pour in the water.
4. Lock the lid. Turn the valve to Sealing.
5. Set to 15 minutes of pressure cook.
6. Do a natural release.
7. Transfer the chicken onto a greased baking pan to broil it for 5 minutes.
8. Drain the pot of liquids and add the rice, coconut milk, salt and 2 tsp garlic puree. Mix well.
9. Lock the lid. Turn the valve to Sealing.
10. Set to 5 minutes of pressure cook.
11. Do a natural release.
12. Serve with sliced cucumber, egg or as you wish. Enjoy!

Singapore Curry Noodles

Prep time: 5 minutes

Cooking time: 15 minutes

Servings: 4

NUTRIENTS PER SERVING:

Carbohydrates – 62 g

Fat – 17 g

Protein – 9 g

Calories – 443

INGREDIENTS:

- 3 Tbsp plus 1 Tbsp oil
- 1 Tbsp ginger, minced
- 1 Tbsp garlic, minced
- 1 red onion, sliced
- 2 eggs + ½ tsp salt, beaten
- 2 green chilies, minced
- 4 ounces chicken, cut into small pieces
- 1 tsp turmeric
- 1 tsp coriander powder
- 1½ tsp salt
- 1 Tbsp soy sauce
- ¾ cup water
- 4 to 6 ounces rice vermicelli
- 1 red bell pepper, sliced
- Chopped cilantro
- 2 to 3 Tbsp lime juice plus extra lime to serve

INSTRUCTIONS:

1. Set to Sauté and heat the 3 Tbsp oil.
2. Add the ginger and garlic and cook for 1 minute.
3. Add the onion and cook for 3-4 minutes.
4. Push the mixture to the side and add 1 Tbsp oil.
5. Add the eggs and scramble. Take out most of the eggs and set aside.
6. Add the chilies and the chicken. Mix well.
7. Add the turmeric, coriander powder, salt and soy sauce and give it a stir.
8. Add the rice noodles and water.
9. Set to 1 minute of low pressure.
10. Do a quick release.
11. Add the scrambled eggs and bell pepper.
12. Stir well and close the pot to let the noodles rest for 5 minutes.
13. Serve with chopped cilantro and lime juice.

Congee

Prep time: 10 minutes

Cooking time: 1 hour

Servings: 6

NUTRIENTS PER SERVING:

Carbohydrates – 29 g

Fat – 12 g

Protein – 22 g

Calories – 500

INGREDIENTS:

- 1 cup jasmine rice, rinsed and drained
- 2 cloves garlic
- 1-2 inches fresh ginger, peeled and sliced
- 3 shitake mushrooms, cut into strips
- 2 lb bone-in chicken pieces, skinless
- 7 cups water
- ½ Tbsp salt
- 3 green onions, sliced
- 1 Tbsp soy sauce
- 1 Tbsp toasted sesame oil

INSTRUCTIONS:

1. Put the rice, garlic, ginger, and mushrooms into the pot.
2. Lay chicken over the rice and add water.
3. Lock the lid. Turn the valve to Sealing.
4. Set to Porridge (no need to adjust the time or pressure).
5. Do a natural release.
6. Transfer the chicken to a cutting board. Shred the chicken with forks and remove the bones. Put it back in the pot.
7. Serve with toasted sesame oil, soy sauce and green onions.
8. Enjoy!

Chili Garlic Noodles

Prep time: 5 minutes

Cooking time: 5 minutes

Servings: 4-6

NUTRIENTS PER SERVING:

Carbohydrates – 38 g

Fat – 5 g

Protein – 19 g

Calories – 286

INGREDIENTS:

- ½ cup soy sauce
- 2 Tbsp brown sugar
- 2 Tbsp white vinegar
- 1 Tbsp chili garlic paste
- 1 Tbsp olive oil
- 2 cups water
- 8 oz. uncooked brown rice noodles
- 1 lb. raw chicken breasts, cut into small pieces
- 2 red bell peppers, sliced
- A pinch of peanuts
- A pinch of green onions, chopped

INSTRUCTIONS:

1. Put all the ingredients (except red peppers) into the pot.
2. Set t0 3 minutes of pressure cook.
3. Do a quick-release.
4. Add in the red bell peppers and stir well.
5. Serve with chili garlic paste, green onions and peanuts.
6. Enjoy!

Lo Mein Beef and Broccoli

Prep time: 10 minutes
Cooking time: 22 minutes
Servings: 6

NUTRIENTS PER SERVING:

Carbohydrates – 38 g
Fat – 20 g
Protein – 24 g
Calories – 426

INGREDIENTS:

- 2 Tbsp vegetable oil
- 1 lb. beef chuck sliced thinly, less than ¼ inch thick.
- 5 cups broccoli florets
- ¼ cup soy sauce
- 2 Tbsp ginger, minced
- 2 Tbsp garlic, minced
- 2 cups beef broth
- 2 Tbsp Chinese rice wine Shaoxing
- 2 tsp sesame oil
- 2 tsp oyster sauce
- ¼ tsp white pepper
- ½ tsp crushed red pepper
- 2 Tbsp brown sugar
- 2 cups mushrooms, sliced
- 8 oz dry spaghetti no. 5
- 1½ tsp sesame seeds, toasted

INSTRUCTIONS:

1. Set to Sauté and heat the oil.
2. Brown beef from each side. Remove it to a plate and set aside.
3. Add the oil to the pot and cook the broccoli until it is crisp-tender.
4. Add ½ tsp soy sauce, sauté for 1-2 minutes, take it out and set aside. Cancel.
5. Add the oil, ginger, and garlic. Cook for 1 minute.
6. Add 1 Tbsp of broth to deglaze the pot.
7. Add the broth, rice wine, sesame oil, soy sauce, oyster sauce, white pepper, red pepper, brown sugar, beef, and mushrooms.
8. Divide the spaghetti into 4 batches.
9. Add one batch of noodles to the broth. Lay in a crisscross pattern.
10. Push the noodles down to cover with broth.
11. Lock the lid and set to 8 minutes of high pressure.
12. Do a quick release and add the broccoli.
13. Let the noodles rest for 5-10 minutes.
14. Serve with sesame seeds. Enjoy!

Rice Pilaf

Prep time: 10 minutes

Cooking time: 10 minutes

Servings: 4-6

NUTRIENTS PER SERVING:

Carbohydrates – 43 g

Fat – 4 g

Protein – 4 g

Calories – 220

INGREDIENTS:

- 1¼ c. olive oil
- ⅓ cup vermicelli
- 1 c. white rice, rinsed
- 1½ cup chicken broth
- 1 tsp garlic powder
- ¾ tsp coarse kosher sea salt
- ¼ tsp ground black pepper
- ¼ tsp onion powder
- ¼ tsp paprika
- 1 Tbsp freshly minced parsley

INSTRUCTIONS:

1. Set to Sauté and heat the oil.
2. Add the vermicelli and cook for 2-3 minutes.
3. Add the rice and cook for 3-4 minutes.
4. Add the broth, garlic powder, salt, pepper, onion powder, and paprika.
5. Lock the lid and set the vent to Sealing.
6. Set to 3 minutes of high pressure.
7. Do a natural release.
8. Add in the parsley. Let the rice rest for 5 minutes.
9. Enjoy!

Rice and Vegetables

Prep time: 7 minutes

Cooking time: 20 minutes

Servings: 4

NUTRIENTS PER SERVING:

Carbohydrates – 43 g

Fat – 4 g

Protein – 4 g

Calories – 219

INGREDIENTS:

- 1-1.5 Tbsp butter
- 2 bay leaves
- 1 white onion, diced
- 2 spring onions, chopped
- 4 cloves garlic, minced
- 2 cups basmati rice
- 3 cups bell peppers and carrots, chopped
- 1.5 cups vegetable stock
- 1 cup coconut milk
- 1 tsp white pepper
- ½ tsp nutmeg
- Salt to taste

INSTRUCTIONS:

1. Set to Sauté and melt the butter.
2. Add the bay leaves, onion, and garlic. Cook for 2-3 minutes.
3. Add the rice and mix well.
4. Add the vegetables and give it a stir.
5. Add the stock and coconut milk. Mix.
6. Add the white pepper, nutmeg, and salt.
7. Mix well to combine.
8. Lock the lid. Turn the valve to Sealing.
9. Set to 6 minutes of high pressure.
10. Do a natural release.
11. Stir well once again.
12. Serve with chopped parsley.
13. Enjoy!

Honey Sesame Chicken Noodles

Prep time: 15 minutes

Cooking time: 20 minutes

Servings: 4

NUTRIENTS PER SERVING:

Carbohydrates – 41 g

Fat – 14 g

Protein – 25 g

Calories – 393

INGREDIENTS:

- 1-2 chicken breasts, diced
- ¼ cup honey
- ¼ cup low-sodium soy sauce
- 1 Tbsp ginger
- 4 cloves garlic, minced
- 1-2 tsp Sriracha
- 1 Tbsp sesame oil
- ½ package rice noodles
- 1½ cups water
- ½ red + yellow pepper, chopped
- 3 broccoli florets
- 1 Tbsp sesame seeds, toasted

INSTRUCTIONS:

1. Add all the ingredients except sesame seeds to the pot.
2. Place the noodles on top of the other ingredients above the liquid.
3. Set to 3 minutes of high pressure.
4. Do a quick-release and turn the vent to Venting.
5. Don't open the lid for 5 minutes to let the noodles sit.
6. Serve with toasted sesame seeds.
7. Enjoy!

LENTILS, GRAINS AND BEANS

Thai Lentil Chickpea Curry

Prep time: 5 minutes

Cooking time: 25 minutes

Servings: 5

NUTRIENTS PER SERVING:

Carbohydrates – 27 g

Fat – 3 g

Protein – 11 g

Calories – 177

INGREDIENTS:

- 1 Tbsp coconut oil
- 2 green onions, chopped
- 1 Tbsp fresh ginger, grated
- 4 cloves garlic, minced
- 1 Tbsp red curry paste
- 12 cherry tomatoes, halved
- 1 14oz can coconut milk
- 1 cup brown lentils, rinsed and drained
- 1 can chickpeas, rinsed and drained
- ½ cup water
- ½ tsp kosher salt

INSTRUCTIONS:

1. Set to Sauté and heat the oil.
2. Add the green onions (only the white stalk), ginger and garlic. Cook for 2-3 minutes.
3. Add the curry paste and tomatoes. Cook for 3 minutes, stirring frequently.
4. Add the coconut milk, lentils, chickpeas, water and salt. Press Cancel.
5. Lock the lid. Turn the valve to Sealing.
6. Set to 6 minutes of high pressure.
7. Do a natural release.
8. Serve hot. Enjoy!

Creamy Red Curry Lentil

Prep time: 5 minutes

Cooking time: 10 minutes

Servings: 5

NUTRIENTS PER SERVING:

Carbohydrates – 46 g

Fat – 7 g

Protein – 16 g

Calories – 325

INGREDIENTS:

- 1 Tbsp avocado oil
- 1 cup onion, chopped
- 1 Tbsp garlic, minced
- 2 carrots, chopped into 1-inch pieces
- 5 Tbsp red curry paste
- 2 cups red lentils
- ½ can diced tomatoes
- 1 can lite coconut milk
- 2 cups vegetable broth
- A pinch of cilantro, chopped

INSTRUCTIONS:

1. Set to Sauté and heat the oil.
2. Add the onion, garlic, and carrots. Cook for 6-8 minutes.
3. Add the red curry paste and lentils. Cook for 1-3 minutes, stirring. Lentils must be covered in paste and oil. Turn off.
4. Add the rest of the ingredients and mix well.
5. Set to 8 minutes of pressure cook.
6. Season to taste with salt and pepper.
7. Serve with chopped cilantro.
8. Enjoy!

Chana Masala

Prep time: 10 minutes
Cooking time: 1 hour 10 minutes
Servings: 6

NUTRIENTS PER SERVING:

Carbohydrates – 29 g
Fat – 16 g
Protein – 8 g
Calories – 281

INGREDIENTS:

- 3 Tbsp vegetable oil, divided
- 1 onion, finely chopped
- Water
- 2 tsp yellow or black mustard seeds
- 2 tsp ground coriander
- 2 tsp Garam Masala
- 1 tsp ground cumin
- 2 tsp kosher salt
- 1 tsp ground turmeric
- 2 tsp freshly squeezed lemon juice
- 2 Tbsp garlic, minced
- 1 Tbsp ginger, minced
- 1 serrano chili, minced
- 1 can diced tomatoes
- 2 cups dried chickpeas, rinsed
- 2 cups greens spinach, chopped
- 2 tsp freshly squeezed lemon juice
- 1 cup cilantro, chopped

INSTRUCTIONS:

1. Set to Sauté and heat the oil.
2. Add the onions. Cook for 10 minutes, stirring occasionally, adding 1 Tbsp water.
3. Add the oil and heat it for 1 minute, until simmering.
4. Add the mustard seeds, garam masala, cumin, salt, coriander, and turmeric. Cook for 1 minute.
5. Add the amchur, garlic, ginger, and chili. Sauté for 1 minute.
6. Add the tomatoes, juice and 2 cups of water. Stir well.
7. Add the chickpeas.
8. Lock the lid and set to 35 minutes of high pressure.
9. Do a natural release.
10. Add the chopped greens and water if it's dry.
11. Set to Sauté and let the greens wilt.
12. Serve with chopped cilantro.

Red Lentil and Potato Curry

Prep time: 8 hours
Cooking time: 10 minutes
Servings: 12

NUTRIENTS PER SERVING:

Carbohydrates – 8 g
Fat – 24 g
Protein – 8 g
Calories – 259

INGREDIENTS:

- 1 Tbsp coconut or olive oil
- ½ yellow or white onion, chopped
- 3 garlic cloves, minced
- 1 Tbsp curry powder
- 1 bay leaf
- 1 tsp ground turmeric
- ½ tsp ground paprika
- ½ tsp red chili flakes
- ¼ tsp ground ginger
- ¼ tsp ground cloves
- 2 cups water
- 1 cup dry red lentils
- 1 cup crushed tomatoes
- 2 large potatoes, peeled and cubed
- 1 can (14 oz) full fat coconut milk
- 1 pinch of cilantro, chopped
- 1 pinch of peanuts, chopped
- 1 tsp apple cider vinegar
- Sea salt, to taste

INSTRUCTIONS:

1. Set to Sauté and heat the oil.
2. Add the onion and garlic. Cook for 5-7 minutes.
3. Add the spices, cilantro, and cloves. Cook for 1-2 minutes.
4. Pour in the water, lentils, and tomatoes. Mix well.
5. Set to 15 minutes of high pressure.
6. Do a quick-release.
7. Add the potatoes and coconut milk.
8. Set to 8 minutes of high pressure.
9. Do a quick-release again.
10. Add in the apple cider vinegar. Give it a stir.
11. Serve with chopped cilantro and peanuts.

Lentil Dal

Prep time: 10 minutes

Cooking time: 35 minutes

Servings: 8

NUTRIENTS PER SERVING:

Carbohydrates – 25 g

Fat – 4 g

Protein – 10 g

Calories – 177

INGREDIENTS:

- 1-2 tsp ghee
- ½ yellow onion, minced
- 1 Tbsp ginger, minced
- 3 garlic cloves, minced
- ¼ cup mild curry paste
- 1 tsp ground coriander
- 1 tsp ground cumin
- 1 14 ounce can lite coconut milk
- 5 cups vegetable broth
- 2½ cups split red lentils masoor dal
- 1 pinch of cilantro, chopped
- Salt to taste

INSTRUCTIONS:

1. Set to Sauté and melt the ghee.
2. Add the onion and ginger. Cook for 3-4 minutes.
3. Add the garlic, curry paste, coriander, and cumin. Cook for 1 minute. Press Cancel.
4. Pour in the coconut milk, vegetable broth, and red lentils. Mix well.
5. Lock the lid. Turn the valve to Sealing.
6. Set to 8 minutes of high pressure.
7. Do a natural release.
8. Season with salt if needed.
9. Serve with chopped cilantro.
10. Enjoy!

Green Beans Potato Curry

Prep time: 10 minutes

Cooking time: 10 minutes

Servings: 5

NUTRIENTS PER SERVING:

Carbohydrates – 14 g

Fat – 2 g

Protein – 6 g

Calories – 99

INGREDIENTS:

- 3.5 cups long green beans, chopped into small pieces
- 2 potatoes, peeled and cubed
- 2 tsp cooking oil
- ½ tsp mustard seeds
- ¼ tsp asafoetida
- 3 cloves garlic
- ½ tsp ground turmeric
- ¼ tsp cayenne powder
- 2.5 tsp ground coriander
- ½ tsp ground cumin
- ¼ cup water, divided
- Salt to taste
- Fresh lemon juice to taste
- 1 pinch cilantro, chopped

INSTRUCTIONS:

1. Set to Sauté and heat the oil.

2. Add the mustard seeds, asafoetida, and garlic. Cook for 30 seconds.
3. Add the green beans, potatoes, turmeric, red chili powder, and ¼ tsp salt. Stir well.
4. Add water and mix well.
5. Lock the lid. Turn the valve to Sealing.
6. Set to 2 minutes of high pressure.
7. Do a natural release.
8. Set to Sauté and add the cumin and coriander.
9. Stir and cook uncovered for 2-3 minutes, stirring occasionally.
10. Add the salt and lemon juice to taste.
11. Serve with chopped cilantro.

Kung Pao Chickpeas

Prep time: 10 minutes

Cooking time: 40 minutes

Servings: 4

NUTRIENTS PER SERVING:

Carbohydrates – 19 g

Fat – 2 g

Protein – 5 g

Calories – 120

INGREDIENTS:

- 1 cup dried chickpeas, soaked overnight
- 1 cup water
- ¼ cup soy sauce
- 2 Tbsp rice vinegar
- 1 Tbsp sugar
- 1½ tsp garlic powder
- 1 tsp onion powder
- ½ tsp ginger powder
- 1 tsp red pepper flakes
- 1 can water chestnuts, drained
- 1 cup chopped bell pepper
- 1 celery stalk, chopped
- ½ cup peanuts, roasted
- 1 tsp sesame oil, toasted
- 1 tsp sesame seeds
- 1 pinch of green onion, chopped

INSTRUCTIONS:

1. Put all the ingredients (except the chestnuts, bell pepper, celery talk, and peanuts) into the pot and stir.
2. Lock the lid and set the vent to Sealing.
3. Set to 35 minutes of high pressure.
4. Do a natural release.
5. Set to Sauté and add the chestnuts, bell pepper, celery stalk, and peanuts. Sauté for 5 minutes.
6. Add the sesame oil and serve with sesame seeds and green onion.
7. Enjoy!

Japgokbap – Multigrain Rice

Prep time: 5 minutes

Cooking time: 25 minutes

Servings: 12

NUTRIENTS PER SERVING:

Carbohydrates – 53 g

Fat – 1 g

Protein – 6 g

Calories – 249

INGREDIENTS:

- 2 cup short-grain white rice, not soaked
- 1 cup sweet rice glutinous
- ½ cup Adzuki red beans
- ½ cup Sweet Sorghum
- ½ cup Millet
- ¼ cup Chickpeas
- ¼ cup Black Beans
- 4½ cup water (ratio 1:0.9)
- ¾ tsp sea salt

INSTRUCTIONS:

1. Rinse and drain the rice. Repeat 2-3 times.
2. Drain the beans and grains. Remove the water.
3. Add the white rice, sweet rice, beans, and grains to the pot.
4. Add the water, ¾ tsp salt to the pot.
5. Lock the lid and set to 18 minutes of high pressure.
6. Do a quick release.
7. Fluff rice with forks before serving.
8. Enjoy!

Southern Green Beans

Prep time: 5 minutes

Cooking time: 10 minutes

Servings: 5

NUTRIENTS PER SERVING:

Carbohydrates – 8 g

Fat – 24 g

Protein – 8 g

Calories – 94

INGREDIENTS:

- 4 slices bacon, chopped
- ½ cup onion, chopped
- 1 cup chicken broth
- 1½ pounds green beans, trimmed and cut in half
- ¾ tsp salt
- ½ tsp garlic powder
- ½ tsp pepper
- 1 pinch of red pepper flakes, crushed
- 1 Tbsp butter

INSTRUCTIONS:

1. Set to Sauté and use cooking spray.
2. Add the bacon. Cook to make the bacon crispy.
3. Add the onion. Sauté for 1 minute.
4. Press Cancel and pour in the chicken broth.
5. Add the rest of the ingredients to the pot.
6. Lock the lid and set to 7 minutes of pressure cook.
7. Do a natural and quick-release.
8. Serve hot and enjoy!

Khidhi – Rice and Lentil Porridge

Prep time: 10 minutes
Cooking time: 30 minutes
Servings: 6

NUTRIENTS PER SERVING:

Carbohydrates – 8 g
Fat – 24 g
Protein – 8 g
Calories – 259

INGREDIENTS:

- ¼ cup chana daal, soaked
- ¼ cup Toor daal, soaked
- ¼ cup masoor daal, soaked
- ¼ cup moong daal, soaked
- 1 cup white rice, soaked
- 2 tsp oil or water
- 1 tsp cumin seeds
- 1 Tbsp ginger
- ½ cup mix of frozen green beans, corn, peas, carrot
- 1 potato and tomato, chopped
- 1 cup cauliflower, chopped
- 2 small green chilis, chopped
- 2 bay leaves
- ½ tsp ground turmeric powder and red chili powder
- 2 tsp salt
- Pinch black pepper
- ¼ cup cilantro optional garnish
- 6 cups water

INSTRUCTIONS:

1. Set to Sauté and heat the oil.
2. Add all of the vegetables. Cook for 5 minutes.
3. Add the bay leaves, turmeric, salt, black pepper, red chili, cumin, and ginger. Sauté for 2-3 minutes.
4. Add the rice, lentils, and water and mix well.
5. Lock the lid. Turn the valve to Sealing.
6. Set to 12 minutes of Rice.
7. Do a natural release.
8. Serve with chopped cilantro.
9. Enjoy!

VEGETARIAN MEALS

Thai Green Curry with Tofu

Prep time: 10 minutes

Cooking time: 10 minutes

Servings: 4

NUTRIENTS PER SERVING:

Carbohydrates – 17 g

Fat – 24 g

Protein – 15 g

Calories – 361

INGREDIENTS:

- 1 can Coconut Milk
- ½ can Maesri Thai Green Curry Paste
- ¼ cup water
- 1 cup baby corn, cut
- 1 cup carrots, chopped
- 1 lb. extra-Firm Tofu cut in ¾ inch pieces
- 2 tsp Brown Sugar
- ½ tsp lime juice
- Thai basil leaves for garnish
- Water

INSTRUCTIONS:

1. Set to Sauté and add the coconut milk, water, and curry paste. Mix well to combine.
2. Add the baby corn, carrots, and Tofu pieces. Stir everything. Let it simmer for a while.
3. Lock the lid. Turn the valve to Sealing.
4. Set to 2 minutes of low pressure.
5. Do a quick-release.
6. Add in the brown sugar and lime juice.
7. If you want the sauce thicker, set to Sauté and cook for 2-3 minutes.
8. Serve with rice and basil leaves.
9. Enjoy!

Lentil and Sweet Potato Thai Curry

Prep time: 15 minutes

Cooking time: 15 minutes

Servings: 4

NUTRIENTS PER SERVING:

Carbohydrates – 20 g

Fat – 5 g

Protein – 5 g

Calories – 142

INGREDIENTS:

- 1 Tbsp olive oil
- 1 14-oz can diced tomatoes + juices
- 1 14-oz can coconut milk
- ½ tsp onion powder
- ½ tsp garlic powder
- 2 cups peeled and diced sweet potato, diced into ¾ inch cubes
- 2 Tbsp red curry paste
- 1-2 tsp sriracha hot sauce
- ½ cup red split lentils
- 3 cups chopped cauliflower
- 3 large handfuls baby spinach
- Salt and pepper, to taste
- 1 pinch of chopped cilantro
- A squeeze of lime juice

INSTRUCTIONS:

1. Add all ingredients to the pot (except the lentils and spinach). Mix well to combine.
2. Add the lentils. Don't stir it to prevent sticking. Push down the lentils to cover them with liquid.
3. Lock the lid and set the vent to Sealing
4. Set to 5 minutes of high pressure.
5. Do a quick-release and turn the vent to Venting.
6. Add in the spinach. Let it rest for a few minutes to make the spinach wilt.
7. Serve with squeezed lime juice and chopped cilantro. Enjoy!

Split Pea Soup

Prep time: 5 minutes

Cooking time: 15 minutes

Servings: 6

NUTRIENTS PER SERVING:

Carbohydrates – 30 g

Fat – 3 g

Protein – 9 g

Calories – 181

INGREDIENTS:

- 1 onion, diced
- 2 ribs celery, diced
- 2 carrots, diced
- 3 cloves garlic, minced
- 1 Tbsp fresh thyme
- 1 bay leaf
- 8 cups vegetable stock
- 2 cups split peas

INSTRUCTIONS:

1. Set to Sauté and heat the oil.
2. Add the onions, celery, and carrots.
3. Add the salt, pepper and cook for 5 minutes.
4. Add the garlic, thyme, bay leaf, stock, and split peas to the pot. Mix well.
5. Lock the lid. Turn the valve to Sealing.
6. Set to 15 minutes of high pressure.
7. Do a quick-release.
8. Serve hot.
9. Enjoy!

Vegetable Chow Mein

Prep time: 10 minutes

Cooking time: 10 minutes

Servings: 5

NUTRIENTS PER SERVING:

Carbohydrates – 23 g

Fat – 4 g

Protein – 7 g

Calories – 145

INGREDIENTS:

- 16 oz Hakka noodles
- 1 cup snow peas, trimmed
- 1 cup cabbage, thinly sliced
- ½ cup celery, chopped
- ½ cup green onion
- ½ cup bell peppers, thinly sliced
- 2 carrots, peeled and sliced into matchsticks
- 4 cups veggie broth low sodium
- 1 tsp grated ginger
- 1 tsp grated garlic
- 2 Tbsp dark soy sauce
- 1 tsp sesame oil
- 1 Tbsp vinegar
- 1 Tbsp Sriracha sauce
- 1 Tbsp ketchup
- 1 Tbsp light brown sugar

INSTRUCTIONS:

1. Add the vegetable broth, soy sauce, vinegar, ketchup, sriracha sauce, sesame oil, and brown sugar to a bowl. Mix well.
2. Set to Sauté and add the sauce to the pot.
3. Put the noodles in the pot.
4. Put the ginger, garlic, and vegetables on top (except the snap peas).
5. Set to 5 minutes of high pressure.
6. Do a quick-release and turn the vent to Venting.
7. Mix the noodles with tongs. While stirring, add the snap peas and lock the lid for 1 minute.
8. Serve with sesame seeds and green onion.

Chinese Kale

Prep time: 10 minutes

Cooking time: 10 minutes

Servings: 4-6

NUTRIENTS PER SERVING:

Carbohydrates – 5 g

Fat – 1 g

Protein – 2 g

Calories – 22

INGREDIENTS:

- 1 Tbsp peanut oil
- 3 cloves garlic, sliced
- 1-inch ginger, crushed
- 1 green onion, trimmed and sliced things
- 1 pound kale, cleaned and stems trimmed
- ½ tsp sea salt
- ½ cup water
- 1 Tbsp soy sauce
- 1 Tbsp oyster sauce
- 1 tsp sesame oil, toasted

INSTRUCTIONS:

1. Add the oil, garlic, ginger, and green onion to the pot.
2. Set to Sauté and when it's hot, cook for 3 minutes.
3. Add the kale and stir to coat it with garlic oil.
4. Add the sea salt and pour in water to cover everything.
5. Lock the lid. Turn the valve to Sealing.
6. Set to 5 minutes of high pressure.
7. Do a quick-release.
8. Add the soy sauce, oyster sauce, and sesame oil then give it a stir.
9. Serve and enjoy!

Vegan White Bean Kale Soup

Prep time: 10 minutes

Cooking time: 20 minutes

Servings: 10

NUTRIENTS PER SERVING:

Carbohydrates – 5 g

Fat – 3 g

Protein – 1 g

Calories – 46

INGREDIENTS:

- 2 Tbsp extra virgin olive oil
- ½ white onion, diced
- 2 carrots, diced
- 2 celery stalks, diced
- 5 cloves garlic, chopped
- 1 28 oz can diced tomatoes
- 4 cups reduced-sodium vegetable broth
- 2 15 oz cans white cannellini beans, drain and rinse
- 1 tsp kosher salt
- ½ tsp Italian seasoning
- ¼ tsp crushed red pepper
- 4 cups kale, chopped

INSTRUCTIONS:

1. Set to Sauté and heat the oil.
2. Add the onions, carrots, celery, and garlic. Cook for 3-4 minutes.
3. Add the beans, salt, tomatoes, Italian seasoning, vegetable stock, and crushed red pepper. Press Cancel.
4. Lock the lid. Turn the valve to Sealing.
5. Set to 1 minute of high pressure.
6. Do a natural release and turn the vent to Venting.
7. Add the kale to the pot and close the lid for 5 minutes.
8. Serve hot and enjoy!

Indian Saag Tofu

Prep time: 10 minutes

Cooking time: 5 minutes

Servings: 4-6

NUTRIENTS PER SERVING:

Carbohydrates – 16 g

Fat – 2 g

Protein – 22 g

Calories – 257

INGREDIENTS:

- 1 pound extra-firm tofu, squeezed and cubed
- 5 Tbsp vegetable oil, divided
- 1 medium yellow onion, diced
- 1-inch piece ginger, minced
- 3 cloves garlic, minced
- 1 can diced tomatoes and their liquid
- ¼ cup water
- ½ tsp ground black pepper
- ¼ tsp cayenne pepper
- 1 tsp salt
- 16 ounce frozen chopped spinach
- 2 tsp garam masala
- ¼ cup coconut milk

INSTRUCTIONS:

1. Set to Sauté and heat 4 Tbsp of oil.
2. Add the onion. Cook for 10 minutes.
3. Meanwhile, heat the rest of the oil in a medium nonstick skillet over a medium-high heat.
4. Add the tofu and sear it for 3 minutes, then flip and repeat for the other side. Turn off and set aside.
5. Add the ginger and garlic and cook for 2 minutes.
6. Add in the seared tofu, cayenne pepper, water, tomatoes, black pepper, salt, and frozen spinach and mix well. Press Cancel.
7. Lock the lid. Turn the valve to Sealing.
8. Set to 5 minutes of high pressure.
9. Do a natural release.
10. Add the garam masala and coconut milk.
11. Serve over rice or with naan.
12. Enjoy!

Vegetable Pho Noodle Soup

Prep time: 25 minutes
Cooking time: 1 hour 25 minutes
Servings: 4-6

NUTRIENTS PER SERVING:

Carbohydrates – 54 g
Fat – 9 g
Protein – 16 g
Calories – 352

INGREDIENTS:

- 2 Tbsp olive oil extra virgin
- 1 sweet onion, cut into quarters
- 5 whole star anise pods
- 1 Tbsp fennel seeds
- 1 Tbsp coriander seeds
- 1 cinnamon stick
- ½ Tbsp whole black peppercorns
- 1 cup mixed dried mushrooms
- 1 1-inch cube of ginger, peeled
- ½ tsp Maggi Seasoning Sauce
- 2 celery stalks
- 8 baby carrots
- 3 garlic cloves, unpeeled
- 2 bay leaves
- 1 lb. extra-Firm Tofu cut in ¾ inch pieces
- 2 kaffir leaves
- 1 sweet onion cut into thin quarter rings
- 2 Tbsp cilantro stems finely chopped
- 8 oz shiitake mushrooms stemmed, sliced
- 1 can straw mushrooms, drained

INSTRUCTIONS:

1. Set to Sauté (High) and heat the oil.
2. Add the onion. Cook for 5 minutes.
3. Add the anise pods, cinnamon stick, fennel seeds, black peppercorns, and coriander seeds. Sauté for 2 minutes. Turn off.
4. Pour 8 cups of water into the pot.
5. Add the rest of the ingredients for the stock. Lock the lid.
6. Set to 30 minutes of high pressure.
7. Do a natural release.
8. Remove the solids out into a colander with a skimmer (set over a bowl) and rinse with 2 cups of water. Squeeze the mushrooms.
9. Add the rinsing liquid back into the pot.
10. Rinse the stock through a strainer over a bowl.
11. Clean the inner pot and put back into the pressure cooker. Put the stock back into the pot. Set to Sauté and heat the stock.
12. Add and simmer the onion and cilantro for 10 minutes.
13. Add the mushrooms. Simmer for 5 minutes. Add the rest of the vegetables. Cook for 3 minutes.
14. Serve with your favorite toppings.

Udon Soup

Prep time: 15 minutes

Cooking time: 15 minutes

Servings: 2

NUTRIENTS PER SERVING:

Carbohydrates – 80 g

Fat – 10 g

Protein – 25 g

Calories – 474

INGREDIENTS:

- 1 120 g (4 oz) dried udon noodles

For the broth:
- 3 scallions, divided
- A handful of cilantro, chopped
- 4 slices of fresh ginger
- 1 large clove of garlic, finely diced
- ⅓ long red chili, sliced
- 5 dried or fresh shiitake mushrooms
- ½ cup frozen edamame beans
- 2 Tbsp soy sauce
- 4 cups vegetable stock

For crispy tempeh:
- 5 oz pressed tempeh, sliced into strips
- 1 Tbsp coconut oil
- 1½ Tbsp soy sauce
- 1 Tbsp agave syrup
- Juice of ¼ lime juice

INSTRUCTIONS:

1. Cook the noodles, following the package directions. Set aside.
2. Add all of the broth ingredients to the pot.
3. Lock the lid. Turn the valve to Sealing.
4. Set to 1 minute of high pressure.
5. Do a quick-release.
6. Meanwhile, heat the oil in a frying pan (medium heat).
7. Add the tempeh slices and cook for 2-3 minutes until both sides are crispy.
8. Mix the soy sauce, syrup, lime juice and sprinkle over the tempeh slices. Set aside.
9. Serve with scallions, cilantro lime juice, and crispy tempeh on the side.
10. Enjoy!

Pad Thai

Prep time: 10 minutes
Cooking time: 10 minutes
Servings: 4

NUTRIENTS PER SERVING:

Carbohydrates – 93 g

Fat – 12 g

Protein – 17 g

Calories – 559

INGREDIENTS:

- ½ cup vegetarian fish sauce
- 2 Tbsp fresh lime juice
- 2 Tbsp rice wine vinegar
- 3 Tbsp coconut aminos
- ⅓ cup granulated sugar
- 1 Tbsp vegetable oil
- 1 medium onion, thinly sliced
- 1 large cloves garlic, minced
- 10 ounces pad Thai rice noodles
- 12 ounces extra-firm tofu, sliced
- 2 cups vegetable stock
- 2 Tbsp shredded sweetened radish
- 1 cup broccoli florets
- 1 carrot, peeled and shaved into ribbons
- 2 large eggs
- ¼ cup peanuts, chopped roasted
- 1 medium lime, cut into 8 wedges

INSTRUCTIONS:

1. Mix the fish sauce, lime juice, coconut aminos, vinegar, and sugar in a bowl.
2. Set to Sauté and heat the oil.
3. Add the onion and cook for 2-3 minutes.
4. Add the garlic and cook for 30 seconds.
5. Pour the fish sauce into onions and garlic.
6. Add the rice noodles and tofu to the pot.
7. Add the stock and radishes. Do not stir.
8. Push the noodles down as much as possible.
9. Lock the lid. Turn the valve to Sealing.
10. Set to 3 minutes of high pressure.
11. Do a quick-release.
12. Add the broccoli and carrots to the pot. Close the lid for 5 minutes.
13. Make scrambled eggs in a small frying pan.
14. Add eggs into the pad Thai.
15. Serve with lime wedges.

DESSERTS

Tsubu-An – Red Bean Paste

Prep time: 15 minutes

Cooking time: 45 minutes

Servings: 24

NUTRIENTS PER SERVING:

Carbohydrates – 7 g

Fat – 4 g

Protein – 7 g

Calories – 80

INGREDIENTS:

- ½ cups uncooked adzuki beans, rinsed and drained
- 5 cups water
- 1¼ cups granulated sugar
- 1 pinch kosher salt

INSTRUCTIONS:

1. Add the beans and water to the pot.
2. Lock the lid. Turn the valve to Sealing.
3. Set to 25 minutes of Bean/Chili.
4. Do a natural release.
5. Remove the foam on the surface of the liquid, and drain the liquid from the beans through a sieve.
6. Put the drained beans back into the pot and add sugar and salt.
7. Set to Sauté (Low) and cook, stirring, until the mixture gets thicker and the sugar has dissolved.
8. Turn off and transfer the tsubu-an to a rimmed baking sheet to cool and thicken.
9. Serve or keep in the fridge or freezer.

Yaksik – Sticky Rice Dessert

Prep time: 1 hour

Cooking time: 30 minutes

Servings: 6

NUTRIENTS PER SERVING:

Carbohydrates – 102 g

Fat – 7 g

Protein – 5 g

Calories – 497

INGREDIENTS:

- 2 cups sweet sticky rice, rinsed and soaked + drained
- 1 cup water
- ½ cup light brown sugar up to ⅔ cup
- 2 Tbsp soy sauce
- 2 Tbsp sesame oil
- ½ cup dried jujube dates, rinsed and into small pieces
- 1 Tbsp pine nuts
- 13 oz Korean chestnuts canned in syrup, cut into quarters.

INSTRUCTIONS:

1. Pour in the sesame oil to coat the bottom.
2. Add the drained sweet rice.
3. Add the soy sauce, sugar and water. Stir a few times to mix everything.
4. Add the chestnuts, jujube and pine nuts.
5. Lock the lid. Turn the valve to Sealing.
6. Set to 8 minutes of low pressure.
7. Do a natural release.
8. Stir the cooked sticky rice with a wooden spoon to mix well.
9. Make sure to mix the bottom too.
10. Leave it for 5-10 minutes.
11. Serve warm and enjoy!

Tapioca Pudding

Prep time: 5 minutes

Cooking time: 15 minutes

Servings: 5

NUTRIENTS PER SERVING:

Carbohydrates – 94 g

Fat – 0.1 g

Protein – 0.1 g

Calories – 369

INGREDIENTS:

- 1 cup small or medium tapioca pearls
- 1 cup water
- 3 cups Almond milk
- ¼ cup Raw sugar
- ⅛ tsp salt
- 1 tsp Vanilla Extract

INSTRUCTIONS:

1. Spray the pot with cooking oil.
2. Add the Tapioca pearls, milk, water and sugar to the pot. Give it a quick stir.
3. Lock the lid. Turn the valve to Sealing.
4. Set to 5 minutes of high pressure.
5. Do a natural release.
6. Add the vanilla and salt and mix well to combine.
7. Serve at room temperature or chilled.
8. Enjoy!

Japanese Cotton Cheesecake

Prep time: 35 minutes
Cooking time: 1 hour
Servings: 8

NUTRIENTS PER SERVING:

Carbohydrates – 10 g
Fat – 7 g
Protein – 6 g
Calories – 127

INGREDIENTS:

- 3 large eggs
- 120 grams cream cheese
- 120 grams white chocolate candy bar

INSTRUCTIONS:

1. Separate the egg whites from the yolks and put the egg whites into fridge.
2. Put the beaters from the mixer into the freezer.
3. Break up the chocolate bar and put in a bowl and cover with foil.
4. Pour in 2 cups of water into the pot and put a trivet inside. Put the bowl on top of the trivet.
5. Lock the lid. Turn the valve to Sealing.
6. Set to 5 minutes of high pressure.
7. Do a quick-release.
8. Take out the bowl and leave trivet inside.
9. Take out the beaters from freezer and the egg whites from the fridge.
10. Whip into Medium Hard Peaks. Put them back in the refrigerator, until needed.
11. Whisk the cream cheese until smooth, carefully add the melted white chocolate and blend to make it smooth.
12. Whisk the egg yolks and chill them.
13. Add a bit of the warm cream cheese mixture to the beaten eggs and whisk.
14. Gradually pour the cream cheese mixture in the cooled egg yolks and blend until smooth.
15. Fold in cold egg whites with a spatula, one-third at a time.
16. Line a cheesecake pan with a parchment round. Take a strip of parchment paper to line around the pan sides.
17. Pour the cheesecake mixture into the pan and place on the trivet.
18. Fold four vertical slits of parchment over the top of the cheesecake.
19. Lock the lid. Turn the valve to Sealing.
20. Set to 15 minutes of high pressure.
21. Do a quick-release.
22. Let cheesecake chill for an hour.
23. Put into the fridge overnight.
24. Serve with powdered sugar on top.

Jello Mochi

Prep time: 5 minutes

Cooking time: 45 minutes

Servings: 6

NUTRIENTS PER SERVING:

Carbohydrates – 31 g

Fat – 0 g

Protein – 1 g

Calories – 132

INGREDIENTS:

- 1 cup mochiko
- 1 package any flavored gelatin
- 1 cups sugar
- 1 cup hot water (not boiling)

INSTRUCTIONS:

1. Mix the mochiko, gelatin and sugar in a bowl.
2. Mix all of the dry ingredients.
3. Pour hot water into the dry ingredients. Stir until smooth.
4. Use a cooking spray to grease a pan and pour in the batter.
5. Pour in 1 cup of water to the pot and place on the trivet.
6. Cover with aluminum foil.
7. Set to 35 minutes of manual.
8. Do a natural release.
9. Take the jello mochi out of the pot and let it cool down.
10. Cut into pieces, using a plastic knife.
11. Roll each piece in potato starch.
12. Serve and enjoy!

Chana Dal Kheer

Prep time: 10 minutes

Cooking time: 10 minutes

Servings: 4

NUTRIENTS PER SERVING:

Carbohydrates – 22 g

Fat – 10 g

Protein – 13 g

Calories – 260

INGREDIENTS:

- ½ cup moong dal
- ¼ cup chana dal
- 2 cups water
- 1 cup jaggery
- 4 cardamom pods, crushed
- A pinch of saffron
- 1 cup milk cow milk
- 5 numbers almonds, crushed
- 10 numbers raisins
- 1 Tbsp ghee

INSTRUCTIONS:

1. Set to Sauté and melt the ghee.
2. Add the almond and raisins. Cook for 1 minute.
3. Add the moong dal and chana dal and sauté until it's golden brown.
4. Add water and put the trivet inside.
5. Put the pot with the jaggery + little water on a trivet.
6. Lock the lid. Turn the valve to Sealing.
7. Set to 10 minutes of manual.
8. Do a natural release.
9. Set to Sauté and add the jaggery syrup to the main pot and give it a stir.
10. Add the milk and saffron strands. Cook for 1 minute.
11. Serve and enjoy!

Gajar Halwa

Prep time: 15 minutes

Cooking time: 30 minutes

Servings: 4

NUTRIENTS PER SERVING:

Carbohydrates – 46 g

Fat – 14 g

Protein – 5 g

Calories – 323

INGREDIENTS:

- 2.5 Tbsp ghee, divided
- 7-8 raw pistachios, broken
- 1 Tbsp golden raisins
- 8 large carrots, grated by hands
- ¾ cup whole milk
- ½ cup granulated white sugar
- ¼ cup milk powder
- ¼ tsp cardamom powder

INSTRUCTIONS:

1. Set to Sauté and melt the ghee.
2. Add the cashews and raisins to the pot. Cook until they become golden. Transfer to a plate and set aside.
3. Add the grated carrots. Cook for 2 minutes.
4. Add whole milk. Mix well.
5. Lock the lid and set the vent to Sealing.
6. Set to 4 minutes of high pressure.
7. Do a natural release.
8. Stir the halwa and set to Sauté.
9. Add the sugar and cook for 3 minutes, stirring.
10. Add the milk powder. Cook for 4 minutes, stirring.
11. Add 1.5 Tbsp ghee to the pot and stir.
12. Cook for another 9 minutes.
13. Add the cardamom powder. Mix well.
14. Add the raisins to the pot. Give it a stir.
15. Serve the halwa with crushed or chopped pistachios. Enjoy!

Kakaland

Prep time: 5 minutes
Cooking time: 25 minutes
Servings: 6

NUTRIENTS PER SERVING:

Carbohydrates – 14 g
Fat – 6 g
Protein – 4 g
Calories – 128

INGREDIENTS:

- ½ gallon milk
- 4 Tbsp vinegar
- 2 cup fresh paneer, rinsed
- ½ cup sugar
- ¾ cup milk
- ¼ cup evaporated milk
- 2 tsp saffron
- 2 tsp ground cardamom
- 2 Tbsp chopped pistachios

INSTRUCTIONS:

1. Pour the milk into the pot.
2. Set to Yogurt and wait until it shows Boil.
3. Lock the lid. Turn the valve to Sealing.
4. When the milk has boiled, open the lid.
5. Pour in the vinegar and give it a good stir.
6. The milk solids and whey will separate. Strain the milk solids using the strainer.
7. Put a weight on top for 2 hours to squeeze all the excess liquid out of the paneer.
8. Set Sauté and pour the milk into the pot.
9. Add the paneer when the milk starts heating up.
10. Stir and let it boil for 2 minutes.
11. Add the evaporated milk and sugar and mix to combine.
12. Stir occasionally and cook until the liquids evaporate.
13. Add the pistachios, saffron, and cardamom powder. Mix well.
14. Continue cooking until all liquids evaporate.
15. Put it in a tray to make a layer about 1 cm high.
16. Cool down the Kakaland and cut into pieces. Enjoy!

Chinese Turnip Cake

Prep time: 25 minutes
Cooking time: 55 minutes
Servings: 10

NUTRIENTS PER SERVING:

Carbohydrates – 15 g

Fat – 4 g

Protein – 2 g

Calories – 120

INGREDIENTS:

- 2 daikon Chinese turnips, peeled and shredded
- 1 pack Chinese sausages, cut into pieces
- ¼ cup dry shrimps, soaked and chopped
- 4 Tbsp olive oil
- 1 tsp ginger, minced
- 2 Tbsp green onion, chopped
- 1½ tsp salt
- ½ tsp sugar
- ¼ tsp chicken bouillon powder
- 1½ cups rice flour
- 1 cup water

INSTRUCTIONS:

1. Set to Sauté and heat the oil.
2. Add green onion and ginger. Cook for 30 seconds.
3. Add the sausage and shrimp. Cook for 1 minute.
4. Add the daikon. Cook for 1-2 minutes.
5. Add the rest ingredients. Sauté for 5 minutes. Set aside and let it cool.
6. Combine the rice flour and water in a bowl.
7. Pour into the cooked turnips and mix.
8. Pour the batter into a medium size oven safe glass pan.
9. Pour water up to the pot's 2 cup mark and put the steam rack inside.
10. Put the glass pan on the steam rack.
11. Lock the lid. Turn the valve to Sealing.
12. Set to 45 minutes of Steam.
13. Do a natural and quick-release.
14. Take out the turnip cakes and set aside to let it cool for a few hours.
15. Take the cake out off the glass pan using a knife.
16. Slice the cake and fry it in a pan with oil to light brown both sides.
17. Serve and enjoy!

Nian Gao – Chinese New Year Cake

Prep time: 5 minutes
Cooking time: 10 minutes
Servings: 5

NUTRIENTS PER SERVING:

Carbohydrates – 108 g
Fat – 2 g
Protein – 6 g
Calories – 482

INGREDIENTS:

- 300 grams glutinous rice flour
- A pinch fine sea salt or table salt
- 110 grams wheat starch

Sugar Mixture:
- 3 pieces cane sugar
- 1 piece brown sugar
- 1½ cup cold water

Sesame Coconut Mixture:
- ¾ cup coconut milk
- 1⅓ Tbsp Chinese sesame paste/sauce

Other ingredients:
- 1½ Tbsp vegetable oil

INSTRUCTIONS:

1. Melt the cane sugar and brown sugar in 1½ cups of cold water slowly over medium heat in a small pan. Don't bring it to a boil.
2. Sift the glutinous rice flour, wheat starch, and salt through a strainer into a bowl.
3. Mix the Chinese sesame paste and coconut milk in a bowl.
4. When the sugar has melted, add the sesame coconut mixture to the sugar to cool it down. Stir well.
5. Add the hot coconut sugar mixture to the bowl with the sifted dry ingredients and mix well to combine.
6. Take out the lumps using a fine-mesh strainer.
7. Add the vegetable oil and stir.
8. Wipe the cake pan with vegetable oil.
9. Pour the batter into the cake pan, using a fine-mesh strainer.
10. Put a trivet inside and pour 1 cup of water into the pot. Set to 28 minutes of pressure cook. Let it boil.
11. Put the cake pan on the trivet with a foil sling right away.
12. Set to 28 minutes of high pressure.
13. Do a natural release.
14. Use a chopstick to check if it is done. Nothing should stick to it if the cake is done. Let the cake cool down.
15. Put the cake into the fridge for 4-8 hours.
16. Cut and serve. Enjoy!

DRINKS

Boba Tea

Prep time: 5 minutes

Cooking time: 20 minutes

Servings: 4

NUTRIENTS PER SERVING:

Carbohydrates – 50 g

Fat – 1 g

Protein – 1 g

Calories – 214

INGREDIENTS:

- 1 cup large boba
- 1½ cups water
- ¼ cup sugar

For the Tea:

- 4 cups strong brewed tea
- 1 Tbsp sugar
- ½ cup whole milk
- 1 cup ice cubes

INSTRUCTIONS:

1. Add the boba pearls, water and sugar to the pot.
2. Set to 2 minutes of high pressure.
3. Let it sit for 5 minutes, then do a quick-release.
4. Transfer the boba to a mason jar and let it cool for 15-20 minutes.
5. Mix the tea, sugar, milk and ice cubes. Shake to cool the tea.
6. Serve the boba covered with tea.

Sikhye – Korean Rice Drink

Prep time: 3 hours

Cooking time: 5 hours

Servings: 6-7

NUTRIENTS PER SERVING:

Carbohydrates – 44 g

Fat – 9 g

Protein – 8 g

Calories – 284

INGREDIENTS:

- 250 g malt
- 2.5 l water
- 1 cup sushi rice, rinsed
- ½ + ¼ cup sugar
- Ice cubes for serving

INSTRUCTIONS:

1. Mix the malt +1 l water in a bowl and mix well to combine. Soak for 30 minutes.
2. Add the rest of the water and rub it together with the malt by hand.
3. Strain the mixture into a large bowl.
4. Let the mixture sit for 3 hours.
5. Add the rice and water to the pot. Make sure the rice is covered with water.
6. Lock the lid. Turn the valve to Sealing.
7. Set to 12 minutes of Rice.
8. Do a quick-release. Set aside to cool.
9. Pour the clean part of the malt mixture into another bowl.
10. Add the malt mixture to the rice and close the lid.
11. Set to 4 hours 20 minutes of Keep Warm.
12. Press cancel and set to Sauté for 30 minutes.
13. Add the sugar and boil it.
14. Skim the white foam from the surface.
15. When it's finishes boiling, transfer to a glass container and let it cool.
16. Serve with ice or to taste.

Nourishing Chinese Red Dates Tea

Prep time: 5 minutes

Cooking time: 1 hour

Servings: 2

NUTRIENTS PER SERVING:

Carbohydrates – 20 g

Fat – 0 g

Protein – 1 g

Calories – 79

INGREDIENTS:

- 50 gr dried red dates, rinsed
- 800 ml water

INSTRUCTIONS:

1. Make a few slits in the dates with scissors, cutting around the edge on one end of the date.
2. Add the red dates and water to the pot.
3. Lock the lid. Turn the valve to Sealing.
4. Set to 10 minutes of high pressure.
5. Do a natural release.
6. Serve and enjoy!

Suanmeitang – Sour Plum Drink

Prep time: 1 minute

Cooking time: 40 minutes

Servings: 2-4

NUTRIENTS PER SERVING:

Carbohydrates – 8 g

Fat – 0 g

Protein – 0 g

Calories – 30

INGREDIENTS:

- 18 grams dried smoked plums, rinsed
- 46 grams Chinese dried hawthorn, rinsed
- 6 grams Chinese dried liquorice, rinsed
- 4-5 cups cold water
- 90 - 125 grams Chinese brown sugar in pieces

INSTRUCTIONS:

1. Add all of the ingredients (except the brown sugar) to the pot.
2. Lock the lid. Turn the valve to Sealing.
3. Set to 30 minutes of high pressure.
4. Do a quick-release.
5. Filter all the ingredients using a strainer.
6. Set to Sauté and put the drink back into the pot.
7. Let it boil. Gradually add brown sugar to taste.
8. Pour the sour plum drink into a glass container and cool it down.
9. Put into the fridge.
10. Enjoy!

Chai Tea

Prep time: 5 minutes

Cooking time: 5 minutes

Servings: 6

NUTRIENTS PER SERVING:

Carbohydrates – 8 g

Fat – 1 g

Protein – 1 g

Calories – 32

INGREDIENTS:

- 6 cups water
- ½ inch knob fresh ginger, chopped
- 4 whole cinnamon sticks
- 6 whole cloves
- 6 whole peppercorns
- 10 whole allspice berries
- 8 cardamom pods
- 10 regular tea bags, tags removed
- Sweetener of your choice, to taste

INSTRUCTIONS:

1. Add water, ginger, spices, and tea bags to the pot.
2. Set to 5 minutes of high pressure.
3. Do a natural release.
4. Discard the tea bags and add sweetener.
5. When it has cooled down, strain the drink and put into the fridge.
6. Serve, mixing in non-dairy milk and concentrate to your taste.

Barley Winter Melon Drink

Prep time: 5 minutes

Cooking time: 1 hour

Servings: 6

NUTRIENTS PER SERVING:

Carbohydrates – 0 g

Fat – 7 g

Protein – 0 g

Calories – 133

INGREDIENTS:

- 1½ cup pearled barley, rinsed and drained
- 1 cup candied winter melon
- 8 cups water
- 2 pandan leaves, rinse and knotted
- Sugar to taste
- Leaf

INSTRUCTIONS:

1. Add the barley, candied winter melon, water, and pandan leaves to the pot.
2. Set to Sauté (Low) and let it boil.
3. Simmer the drink for 1 hour.
4. Transfer to a glass decanter and cool down.
5. Serve warm or chilled.

Amazake – Japanese Rice Drink

Prep time: 10 minutes

Cooking time: 10 minutes

Servings: 6

NUTRIENTS PER SERVING:

Carbohydrates – 102 g

Fat – 7 g

Protein – 5 g

Calories – 497

INGREDIENTS:

- 1 cup of uncooked rice, washed
- 1 cup of koji
- Water for cooking the rice
- 1 cup of water

INSTRUCTIONS:

1. Add the rice to the pot. Pour in water until it reaches the 1 cup porridge water line.
2. Set to standard Porridge mode.
3. When it's done, take out the pot from the pressure cooker to cool it down a little.
4. Carefully pour in water to cool down the porridge to 140F.
5. Add the koji. Give it a good stir to combine.
6. Put the bowl back into the pot.
7. Set to 8 hours of manual 140 F.
8. Serve it warm or chilled.

Indian Masala Milk

Prep time: 7 minutes

Cooking time: 14 minutes

Servings: 12

NUTRIENTS PER SERVING:

Carbohydrates – 19 g

Fat – 10 g

Protein – 5 g

Calories – 209

INGREDIENTS:

- 12 cups milk
- ½ cups almonds
- ½ cups cashew nuts
- ½ cup pistachios
- 4 green cardamom
- 1 tsp saffron
- 1 tsp dry ginger powder
- 1½ tsp nutmeg freshly grated

INSTRUCTIONS:

1. Add the pistachios, cashew nuts, and almonds to a blender and make a powder.
2. Mix the ginger powder, nutmeg, and saffron in a bowl.
3. Add both mixtures and milk to the pot.
4. Lock the lid. Turn the valve to Sealing.
5. Set to 14 minutes of high pressure.
6. Do a natural release.
7. Transfer to a decanter and cool it down.
8. Enjoy!

Aam Panna – Raw Mango Drink

Prep time: 10 minutes

Cooking time: 30 minutes

Servings: 6-7

NUTRIENTS PER SERVING:

Carbohydrates – 45 g

Fat – 0 g

Protein – 0 g

Calories – 179

INGREDIENTS:

- 2 unripe green mangoes
- 4 cups water
- ½ cup sugar
- ½ tsp black salt
- ½ tsp roasted cumin powder
- ¼ tsp salt
- Ice cubes
- Fresh mint, garnish

INSTRUCTIONS:

1. Cut small slits in the mangoes with a knife.
2. Pour 2 cups of water into the pot.
3. Put a steamer basket inside and put the mangoes in it.
4. Lock the lid and set the valve to Sealing.
5. Set to 15 minutes of high pressure.
6. Do a quick-release.
7. Cool the mangoes and peel them.
8. Add the pulp, 4 cups of water, sugar, black salt, cumin powder and salt to a blender to make a smooth mixture.
9. Pour the drink into glasses with ice.
10. Serve with sprinkled roasted cumin powder and a fresh sprig of mint.

Shikandji – Indian Lemonade

Prep time: 5 minutes

Cooking time: 5 minutes

Servings: 2

NUTRIENTS PER SERVING:

Carbohydrates – 23 g

Fat – 0 g

Protein – 0 g

Calories – 90

INGREDIENTS:

- Juice of 1 lemon
- 3 Tbsp sugar
- ½ tsp black salt
- 1 inc ginger, grated
- ½ tsp cumin powder
- ½ tsp ground pepper
- Ice cubes
- 2.5 cups water
- 5 mint leaves

INSTRUCTIONS:

1. Add all of the ingredients to the pot.
2. Lock the lid. Turn the valve to Sealing.
3. Set to 8 minutes of high pressure.
4. Do a natural release.
5. Pour into serving glasses and refrigerate.
6. Serve chilled with ice cubes and mint leaves.

CONCLUSION

Thank you for reading this book and having the patience to try the recipes.

I do hope that you have had as much enjoyment reading and experimenting with the meals as I have had writing the book.

Stay safe and healthy!

Recipe Index

A

Aam Panna	144
Amazake	142
Asaam Pedas Fish	85

B

Bacon Ramen	77
Bak Kut Teh	48
Bang Bang Srimp Pasta	95
Banh-Mi	72
Barley Winter Melon Drink	141
Beef Rendang	73
Black Rice Pudding	36
Boba Tea	136

C

Caramelized Pork	71
Cashew Chicken	57
Chai Spice Mix	29
Chai Tea	140
Chana Dal Kheer	131
Chana Masala	108
Chao Ca	80
Chao Ga	96
Char Siu	75
Chawanmushi	37
Chicken Pad Thai	93
Chicken Rice Bowls	94
Chicken Tikka Masaka	62
Chili Garlic Noodles	101
Chinese 5 Spice Mix	27
Chinese Kale	120
Chinese Lemon Sauce	25
Chinese Pork Shoulder Soup	52
Chinese Turnip Cake	134
Coconut Caramel Shrimp	81
Coconut Mahi-Mahi	83
Congee	100
Congee with Bacon	33
Creamy Red Curry Lentil	107
Curry Powder	30

E

Eight Treasure Congee	31

G

Gajar Halwa	132
Galbitang	50
Garam Masala	28
General Tso Chicken	60
Ginger Sauce	22
Green Beans Potato Curry	111

H

Habachi Steak and Vegetables	64
Hainanese Chicken Rice	97
Hibachi Fried Rice	92
Hoisin Sauce	24
Honey Sesame Chicken Noodles	105

I

Indian Butter Shrimp	84
Indian Curry Lamb	76
Indian Masala Milk	143
Indian Saag Tofu	122

J

Japanese Cotton Cheesecake	129
Japanese Fried Rice	91
Japgokbap	113
Jello Mochi	130

K

Kakaland	133
Khidhi	115
Kimchi Jjigae	44
Korean Beef	65
Korean Gochujang Chicken Wings	55
Korean Red Chili Sauce	26
Korean Short Ribs	66
Kung Pao Chicken	61
Kung Pao Chickpeas	112

L

Laksa Soup 49
Lentil and Sweet Potato Curry 117
Lentil Dal 110
Lo Mein Beef and Broccoli 102

M

Mango Chicken 59
Massaman Beef Curry 68
Miso Oatmeal 39
Miso Soup 43
Miyeok Guk 51
Mushroom Ramekin Eggs 38

N

Nasi Lemak 98
Nian Gao 135
Nikujaga 32
Nikujaga 79
Nourishing Chinese Red Dates Tea 138

O

Orange Chicken Lettuce Wraps 63

P

Pad Thai 125
Panko-Crusted Cod 88
Pork Belly Ramen 42
Pork Pho with Bacon 40

Q

Quinoa Breakfast Bowl 34

R

Ramen Soup 41
Red Lentil and Potato Curry 109
Red Lentil Soup 46
Rice and Vegetables 104
Rice Pilaf 103

S

Sambal Udang 89

Shikandji 145
Shrimp Tom Kha 47
Shrimp with Lobster Sauce 90
Sikhye 137
Singapore Curry Noodles 99
Southern Green Beens 114
Split Pea Soup 118
Steamed Fish with Ginger 87
Steamed Sea Bass 86
Suanmeitang 139
Sundubu JJigae 45
Szechuan Beef 74

T

Tahi Sweet Chili Sauce 21
Takikomi Gohan 35
Tandoori Chicken 58
Tapioca Pudding 128
Teriyaki Chicken 53
Teriyaki Sauce 23
Teriyaki Wings 54
Thai Green Curry with Tofu 116
Thai Lemongrass Chicken 56
Thai Lentil Chickpea Curry 106
Tsubu-An 126

U

Udon Soup 124

V

Vegan White Bean Kale Soup 121
Vegetable Chow Mein 119
Vegetable Pho Noodles Soup 123
Vietnamese Beef Pho 69
Vietnamese Bo Kho 70
Vietnamese Caramel Salmon 82
Vietnamese Salmon 78

Y

Yaksik 127
Yukgaejang 67

Conversion Tables

VOLUME EQUIVALENTS (LIQUID)

US STANDARD	US STANDARD (OUNCES)	METRIC
2 tablespoons	1 fl. oz.	30 mL
¼ cup	2 fl. oz.	60 mL
½ cup	4 fl. oz.	120 mL
1 cup	8 fl. oz.	240 mL
1½ cups	12 fl. oz.	355 mL
2 cups or 1 pint	16 fl. oz.	475 mL
4 cups or 1 quart	32 fl. oz.	1 L
1 gallon	128 fl. oz.	4 L

OVEN TEMPERATURES

FAHRENHEIT (°F)	CELSIUS (°C) APPROXIMATE
250 °F	120 °C
300 °F	150 °C
325 °F	165 °C
350 °F	180 °C
375 °F	190 °C
400 °F	200 °C
425 °F	220 °C
450 °F	230 °C

VOLUME EQUIVALENTS (LIQUID)

US STANDARD	METRIC (APPROXIMATE)
⅛ teaspoon	0.5 mL
¼ teaspoon	1 mL
½ teaspoon	2 mL
⅔ teaspoon	4 mL
1 teaspoon	5 mL
1 tablespoon	15 mL
¼ cup	59 mL
⅓ cup	79 mL
½ cup	118 mL
⅔ cup	156 mL
¾ cup	177 mL
1 cup	235 mL
2 cups or 1 pint	475 mL
3 cups	700 mL
4 cups or 1 quart	1 L
½ gallon	2 L
1 gallon	4 L

WEIGHT EQUIVALENTS

US STANDARD	METRIC (APPROXIMATE)
½ ounce	15 g
1 ounce	30 g
2 ounces	60 g
4 ounces	115 g
8 ounces	225 g
12 ounces	340 g
16 ounces or 1 pound	455 g

Other Books by Tiffany Shelton

Tiffany Shelton's page on Amazon